ESSENTIAL

THE COCKTAIL BOOK

A COMPLETE GUIDE TO MODERN DRINKS WITH 150 RECIPES

**EDITED BY
MEGAN KRIGBAUM**

PHOTOGRAPHS BY
DANIEL KRIEGER

TEN SPEED PRESS
California | New York

contents

RECIPE
list.

CLASSIC RECIPES

MODERN RECIPES

INTRODUCTION

Over the course of the past three hundred years of drinking history, since the first punch was made, a solid stable of classic cocktails has emerged. These tried-and-true recipes have endured for their distinctive personalities and winning flavors, but they're also respected for having reliable templates. New York City bartender Sam Ross has said that "classics are the formulas of balance," which is why many of the new drinks seen on bar menus these days have sprung from this old guard: their formulas work. And, thanks to an ever-growing contingent of devoted and creative bartenders, not to mention the outright explosion of craft spirits into the marketplace over the past fifteen years, it is now possible to get a well-made drink in just about any city in the country.

But among the plethora of wittily named drinks made with unlikely combinations of unheard-of ingredients and house-made syrups that has resulted from this renaissance, a conundrum has arisen: which of these drinks are worth keeping around? The best of these modern interpretations are thoughtful revisions of the classics that point to the creativity that can arise from knowing the standards backward and forward. The greatest bartenders will understand a cocktail's personality, history, and intention—not to mention the ingredient ratio that informs it.

In these pages, you'll find 150 recipes—the classics are all here, from the Gimlet to the Old-Fashioned, alongside the best examples of riffs on them, sourced from some of the greatest bartenders of our time. Though there are successful blueprints, you'll notice through these variations that there are no hard-and-fast rules. The truth is, drinks are made to be tinkered with. At the most basic level, the classic recipes are composed of modular building blocks: spirit, perhaps citrus, a little sugar, a dash of bitters. All this means that a drink originally based in whiskey can be completely transformed when made with a core of applejack as long as the rest of the cocktail is appropriately adjusted to remain balanced.

What becomes apparent when looking at these originals and their descendants together are distinct branches of the cocktail family tree that give bartenders a solid jumping-off point for adding their own leaves. As you shake and stir your way through this book, getting the classics down and investigating this selection of outstanding modern updates, hopefully you'll feel moved to improvise based on whatever is in your liquor cabinet. These pages will provide you with the tools—and the permission—to ruminate on the pleasures found in using pineapple rum instead of the usual white to make a daiquiri, tossing a few fresh raspberries into a bramble in the peak of summer, using expensive Japanese "whisky" in an old-fashioned, or even adding dry cider to your gin and tonic.

bar
ESSENTIALS

the cocktail family tree

NO MATTER HOW FAR OUTSIDE the box bartenders go, most drinks are informed by one of the classic templates that makes up each distinct branch of the cocktail family tree. Here's a guide to basic drink categories to springboard from:

PUNCH

The predecessor to most drinks that we know today, large-format drinks were popularized in the eighteenth century, way before their single-serve counterparts. Classic punches rely on a base of five key ingredients: spirit, sugar, water, spice, and citrus.

SOUR

A direct descendant of punch, the classic sour is born from a base spirit (bartender's choice), citrus, sugar, and water, shaken and served in a small glass without ice. Some classic sours include the infamous Whiskey Sour (page 198), the Daiquiri (page 74), and the frothy, egg white–fortified Pisco Sour (page 157).

FIZZ

Essentially a sour (spirit, citrus, sugar) that's shaken and topped off with seltzer or soda water, a fizz is served in a tall glass without ice. Gin is the traditional fizz base, but any spirit will work in this formula. Some of the most well-known fizzes, like the Ramos Gin Fizz (page 163), are made with an egg white, which gives the drink an ethereal, foamy head.

COLLINS

A collins is a longer (that is, bigger) fizz that's built (meaning that it's made in the glass it's served in) over ice, and topped off with soda water. The most well-known drink in this family is the Tom Collins (page 189), but other classics, like the Florodora (page 85) deserve memorizing, too.

COCKTAIL

When the word *cocktail* first came into use (most likely in the early 1800s), it referred to a drink made with spirit, sugar, bitters, and water. Though over time the word has been assigned to every sort of mixed drink, the original definition refers to a family of drinks that includes the Manhattan (page 114), Old-Fashioned (page 142), Martini (page 121), etc.

FLIP

This is one of the oldest families of cocktails. The term appears to have been used as long ago as the late 1600s, describing a combo of beer, rum, and sugar cooked over high heat. By the nineteenth century, the flip had lightened up a bit, made with a spirit or fortified wine and shaken with sugar and an egg, then topped with grated nutmeg. The Sherry Flip (page 175) is a longstanding and excellent example of this family.

SPARKLING

The sparkling category of cocktails has several branches. First, there's the Champagne Cocktail (page 67) and its variations, followed quickly by a class of royales, which simply refer to drinks that are topped with, rather than based on, Champagne or sparkling wine. With origins as an aperitivo, or pre-dinner drink, in northern Italy in the early 1900s, a spritz calls for a bitter liqueur, sparkling wine, and sparkling water all served over ice. This easily transformed template has seen hundreds of iterations, but the best known is the Aperol Spritz (page 41).

JULEP

Even though the julep is notoriously associated with the Kentucky Derby, the old-school Southern recipe of spirit, sugar, and mint served over crushed ice actually predates the race by nearly a hundred years. The exact origins and recipe have no doubt inspired countless dissertations, but, in short, the julep most likely originated in Virginia in the late 1700s, when it was considered an aristocratic drink. Bourbon became the preferred spirit only after the Civil War, when the South was impoverished and, thanks to phylloxera, brandy had all but disappeared.

COBBLER

Dating to the late 1800s, the cobbler is another punch descendent. Its template calls for a combination of a spirit, sugar, crushed ice, and fruit, served with a straw. The most famous member of this family is the Sherry Cobbler (page 173), which has seen a real renaissance with the recently revived interest in sherry. The cobbler is easy to riff on and adaptable to the seasonal fruit at hand. High summer might call for raspberries muddled with lemon, while fall is for cranberries and orange.

TIKI

Originated in 1930s LA by bar owner Donn Beach (a.k.a Don the Beachcomber), tiki cocktails are characterized by their booziness, plethora of ingredients, and over-the-top garnishes. Though they typically include multiple rums in addition to other spirits, and flavors like warm spice, coconut, and tropical fruit, modern renditions also make use of other base sprits and even Amari.

BEER

While shandies, radlers, and micheladas are probably the best-known subsets of the beer cocktail sphere, bartenders have been using beer in drinks, in myriad ways, since the mid-1800s. What probably began as a way to make beer taste better has evolved into a way to make flavorful, lower-alcohol drinks, interesting flavor combinations, and fizzy morning refreshers.

ingredients

EVERY BARTENDER, WHETHER A WORKING pro or a home mixer, needs a well—a stash of spirits that can be used as the base for almost any drink—plus a small arsenal of essential tools and glassware. By no means do you need *all* of these. A basic bar starts with gin, rum, tequila, vodka, and whiskey, and is made better by other spirits that fit the taste of the drink maker and the styles of cocktail they tend to prefer. If you're a tiki lover, don't skip the orgeat. Love a spritz? Invest in a couple of aperitivo liqueurs and amari. If you don't know where to start, use a small menu of classic recipes to guide your shopping in addition to the basics. Here are the must-haves, plus a selection of modifiers that can level-up your cocktail game.

GIN

For a spirit to be considered gin, it has to have, at its most elementary level, a distinct juniper component. Beyond that, gin is not closely regulated; it's made just about everywhere in a slew of different styles that vary widely depending on the botanicals (besides juniper) used in distillation, as well as the amount of sugar added, and the resulting texture.

LONDON DRY GIN The white-button-down classic that's been around since England lost its mind for gin in the nineteenth century. A London dry is clean, dry, juniper-forward, and Martini-ready.

PLYMOUTH GIN Plymouth is defined by its place of origin: Plymouth, England. The style is very similar to a London dry (and can be used interchangeably), but it's fuller bodied with a more earthy botanical mix. Use this when you want to add textural complexity to a gin drink.

OLD TOM GIN Slightly sweet, with a touch of malt flavor, this pre-Prohibition style bridges the gap between genever (see following) and a London dry gin. It's become the go-to among bartenders looking to re-create the classic drinks of that era, especially the Martinez (page 118).

GENEVER Long considered the predecessor to gin, genever originated in Holland in the sixteenth century. It's built from a malted-grain base and has a less prominent botanical component than the crisp, aromatic gin we know today.

SLOE GIN This reddish purple spirit isn't so much a gin as a liqueur made from infusing gin with the tart-sweet juice from sloe plums. Best known for its presence in the Sloe Gin Fizz (page 181), sloe gin can be used in place of any fruit liqueur, especially in cobblers or Champagne cocktails.

AMERICAN The American craft spirit movement has produced a host of idiosyncratic gins that range from citrusy to peppery to floral. "Navy-strength" gins—high-proof gins clocking in around 60% ABV—have also become popular of late.

RUM

Nearly every country in and near the Caribbean makes its own rum. In all cases, a sugarcane derivative serves as the base, be it fresh cane juice, cane syrup, or molasses. This base is fermented and then distilled, in either a pot or column still, and often involves blending distillates from a combination of the two. The amount of time the rum spends in oak barrels after distilling (or, in many cases, the addition of caramel coloring) determines its color and flavor, while geography tends to define the style.

WHITE RUM Clear and dry, aged in neutral oak or steel barrels for a short amount of time, this is the go-to for a Daiquiri (page 74) and a Mojito (page 131).

GOLDEN RUM The pale yellow or gold color is due to time spent in toasted oak barrels, or even the addition of caramel coloring. Barrel-aged examples will have more depth of flavor and a perceived sweetness, and often vanilla or spice notes.

DARK RUM This is much deeper in color than golden rum thanks to extended time in barrels and/or even more caramel coloring. The best barrel-aged dark rums develop concentrated spice, vanilla, and brown sugar notes and can be sipped on their own, like bourbon. The longer they're aged, the more expensive they'll be.

BLACK STRAP RUM Very dark—almost black—in color, this rum gives a very sweet, rich flavor to drinks. Its color comes from the addition of caramel or molasses after fermentation.

RHUM AGRICOLE Grassy and aromatic, Rhum Agricole is made with fresh sugarcane juice that's pressed in the fields where it's harvested and then fermented. Agricole is made in unaged white versions as well as darker aged ones.

TEQUILA

Tequila is made from the center heart, or *piña*, of blue agave plants that grow in Mexico's western Jalisco region, as well as a handful of other Mexican states. The *piña* is harvested and steam-cooked and then the juice is extracted from the plants and fermented before being distilled. By law, the final product must be double stilled (at a minimum) for purity and is subject to a number of aging regulations. Choose a tequila based on the way you like to drink it—be it mixed in cocktails or on its own. In general, blanco tequilas, which are unaged, tend to have more vegetal flavors and are a bit more harsh than aged ones, which means they're best smoothed out in a cocktail; in contrast, añejo tequilas, which are aged for at least a year, develop distinct barrel flavors and are better sipped alone.

BLANCO Also called silver or *plata*, this style of tequila is unaged, which means it's crystal clear, has a fairly neutral flavor, and works well in many cocktails.

REPOSADO This golden-colored tequila is aged two to eleven months in barrels, where it picks up very subtle woody flavors.

AÑEJO Aged in wood barrels between one and three years, añejo tequilas are smoother and have deeper wood flavors. The cost and complexity of this style of tequila makes it best suited to sipping rather than mixing.

MEZCAL

Technically, tequila is a subset of mezcal and not the other way around. Mezcal often has a distinctly smoky flavor because the agave used to make it is roasted over stones and wood rather than being steamed.

VODKA

By definition, vodka is colorless and flavorless—qualities that helped it earn the distinction of the bartender's least-favorite spirit. Gradually, the tide has turned, and now bartenders appreciate vodka for its ambiguous but high-octane character, which can help amplify flavors in a drink. High-proof vodka (more than 100 proof) is particularly useful in this way. Vodka can be distilled from just about anything: wheat, potatoes, apples, and quinoa, to name a few.

WHISKEY

Given the number of distinct whiskey varieties available, it would be easy to fill an entire bar with just this spirit. Many regions of the world are known for making whiskies from fermented grain mash, but the grains and distilling methods used vary widely from one place to the next. For most cocktail making purposes, it's recommended you have a good bourbon, rye, and Scotch on hand, as each will add a distinct character to a mixed drink.

BOURBON The mostly widely recognized American variety of whiskey, bourbon is distilled from a fermented mash that contains at least 51 percent corn. When first distilled, whiskey is clear; it picks up its color and toasty, vanilla flavors with barrel aging. Bourbon often has a little bit of a sweet note to it, which means that it can be more approachable than Scotch.

RYE This American whiskey must be distilled from a fermented mash that contains at least 51 percent rye grain. Rye tends to be a little spicier and more assertive than bourbon.

SCOTCH The Scottish make their "whisky" (they omit the "e" in their spelling) from malted barley. Most of the variation in Scotch is based on where it is made and the malt or grains used. For instance, Islay scotches, which are made from grain that's smoked over peat, tend to be a little smoky, whereas Highland scotches tend to be much bigger and broader on the palate.

JAPANESE WHISKY Whiskey has been made in Japan since the 1920s, but it wasn't until the 1930s, after Masetsaka Takesuru returned from a several years—long apprenticeship at a Scotch distillery, that the Japanese really stepped up their game—and adopted the Scotch spelling. It has only been in the past ten years that this style has gotten much attention in the United States, but these whiskeys tend to be exceptional, and made in a single-malt style with extended barrel aging.

BRANDY

Brandy is a spirit that's distilled from fermented fruit juice or fruits. The most famous are Cognac and Armagnac from France, and these are distilled from grapes. Legally, brandy must be distilled at less than 190 proof and bottled at more than 80 proof.

COGNAC AND ARMAGNAC The best of these brandies, distilled from grapes in the Charentes region of France, can be quite expensive; thus, they tend to be best enjoyed neat—with nothing else in the glass to distract. But Cognac also plays an important role in cocktails such as the Sidecar (page 177) and the French 75 (page 86), and a number of distillers make a more affordable option for this purpose.

PISCO Chile and Peru love to bicker over which country made this clear grape brandy first. Whatever the case, pisco doesn't turn up in a ton of cocktails, but it's good to have around for making frothy Pisco Sours (page 157).

EAU-DE-VIE Eau-de-vie is made by distilling fermented fruit, like pears (*poire*), cherries (*kirsch*), and raspberries (*framboise*). Unlike fruit liqueurs, eaux-de-vie are not sweetened, which means you'll often need to add sugar when using them in drinks.

AQUAVIT

Aquavit is a Scandinavian spirit that has a lot in common with gin, but rather than having juniper as its essential flavor element, aquavit is based in caraway that's blended with other herbs and spices. Use aquavit as you would gin or vodka. It's outstanding in a Bloody Mary (page 56).

CACHAÇA

Distilled from sugarcane juice and traditionally bottled without aging, cachaça is essentially Brazil's take on rum and it's crucial to the country's most popular drink, the Caipirinha (page 64). This white spirit can be used in any drink that typically calls for white rum.

SHERRY

A classic fortified wine from Spain's southern Jerez region, sherry is made in a number of different styles. The lightest, fino sherry, is crisp and salty and unaged; you'll understand why it goes so well with citrus and other vibrant flavors. Amontillado and oloroso sherries, while dry, have more flavors of dried fruits and nuts thanks to extended oxidation.

VERMOUTH

A fortified wine that's traditionally made bitter with wormwood and aromatized with other spices and herbs, the best vermouth has historically been made in Europe. Generally speaking, vermouth comes in three styles: sweet or red, blanc or white, and dry. An important ingredient in many classic cocktails, it can also be served on its own, over ice.

SWEET OR ROSSO This style originated in Torino (Turin), Italy, in the late 1700s. Spicy and fruity, sweet vermouth is necessary to many cocktails, the most famous of which are the Manhattan (page 114) and the Negroni (page 135).

BLANC OR BIANCO Based in white wine, blanc vermouth originated in Chambery, France, and is also made with a touch of sugar, giving this floral aperitif a nice smooth texture.

DRY Originally from Marseilles, France, "dry" vermouth has minimal residual sugar, is based in white wine, and is just what you want to balance a Martini (page 121).

APERITIF WINES

These relatively low-ABV aromatized wines are infused with herbs, roots such as wormwood or gentian, citrus peels, and other botanicals. Many aromatized wines, including vermouth and quinqina, are additionally fortified with neutral spirits, often grape brandy, putting them between 14 and 20 percent alcohol.

LILLET This aperitif wine brand from France comes in white, rosé, and red versions. It's infused with citrus and very subtle herb flavors, and is often served over ice with a slice of orange. But it can also act much like blanc vermouth in martini-style drinks like the Vesper (page 193) and the Corpse Reviver No. 2 (page 73).

BONAL Infused with gentian, cinchona (quinine), and other herbs, this aperitif has been made in the Jura Mountains in southwest France since 1865. Great in a spritz or a Champagne cocktail, it is also a nice substitute for gin in a super-bitter Gin and Tonic (page 95).

BYRRH QUINQUINA Made in southwest France, this is a classic example of quinquina, a family of aperitif wines seasoned with quinine. Byrrh is a solid match with gin and can substitute for sweet vermouth in a Negroni (page 135) or be used as the base for a gin cobbler.

COCCHI AMERICANO Made in Italy's Torino (Turin) region, Cocchi Americano is made from Moscato d'Asti grapes and is flavored with gentian and other herbs.

LIQUEURS

Made by macerating fruit, flowers, or herbs in a distilled neutral spirit and then sweetening with sugar, liqueurs are typically used in cocktails in small amounts to add aromatic complexity and to balance sweetness. They tend to fall into two larger categories based on flavor and use: those that are fruity or floral, and those that are herbal or bitter.

ORANGE LIQUEURS There are two main styles of orange liqueurs: triple sec and curaçao. The best known brand of curaçao, which tends to be heavier and sweeter than triple sec, is Grand Marnier; Cointreau is the most widely recognized triple sec. Other great versions are Combier and Pierre Ferrand Dry Curaçao.

MARASCHINO This Italian liqueur, made from Marasca cherries, has a far more herbal character than its name implies. Most bartenders prefer the maraschino that's made by the Luxardo family.

CHERRY HEERING More spiced than herbal, this cherry liqueur was created in the 1700s by a Dane named Peter Heering. More dark cherry-forward than maraschino, it is the cherry of choice for a Singapore Sling (page 178) or a Blood and Sand (page 55).

CRÈME DE CASSIS This French black currant-flavored liqueur is mainly known for its role in the classic Kir Royale, but it's also a superb off-season substitute for fresh fruit in cobblers.

CRÈME DE VIOLETTE A deep-purple liqueur that's flavored with violet blossoms, crème de violette is key to the classic Aviation (page 42) cocktail.

ST-GERMAIN This elderflower-infused liqueur has been around for only about ten years, but it quickly became a favorite of bartenders for use in gin- and Champagne-based cocktails. It also works well in drinks flavored with ginger, like the Go-To (page 252).

ABSINTHE A French creation, absinthe is traditionally made with anise, fennel, and wormwood. Outlawed in the United States for nearly a century (1912 to 2007), it's now available for use as a key component in classic cocktails such as the Sazerac (page 168) and Death in the Afternoon (page 82).

CHARTREUSE The recipe for Chartreuse, originally produced by a Carthusian monastery in the eighteenth century and purportedly containing 130 different herbs, has remained a tightly held secret by generations of monks. The green variety is 110 proof and more highly spiced, while the yellow is only 80 proof and has a much sweeter profile. Find Chartreuse in the Last Word (page 111) or the frozen Piña Verde (page 297).

SUZE This Swiss aperitif is flavored with gentian root, which gives it a citrusy, bitter flavor. For many years, Suze wasn't available in the States, but it's been here and put to good use for the past five years in drinks like the White Negroni (page 327).

APERITIVO LIQUEURS

The Italians have a long history of making exceptional bitter liqueurs, or *aperitivi*. Thanks to drinks such as the Negroni (page 135) and Aperol Spritz (page 41), apertivos like Campari, Aperol, and Cappelletti have become hugely popular in the States in the past ten years. But these spirits also turn up in drinks like the Boulevardier (page 59), paired with whiskey, and even in tiki-style cocktails, like the Jungle Bird (page 108).

AMARO

Amari are the complement to *aperitivi*: bitter *digestivo* (post-meal) liqueurs ranging from 30 to 60 percent ABV. Amaro is made by infusing a neutral spirit with a selection of herbs, roots, spices, and dried fruits, then sweetening it and aging in barrels. Amaro mixes well with darker spirits, including whiskey, aged rum, and toffee-scented oloroso sherry, because of its plethora of fruit and spice notes.

AROMATIZED BITTERS

About five years ago, the bitters universe exploded with artisan producers making flavors that had never been seen before in this category. An infusion of high-proof alcohol with herbs, spices, roots, bark, and other ingredients, bitters are super concentrated and add a nice kick of flavor to a drink. There are three basics that turn up most often in cocktail recipes:

ANGOSTURA Created by a doctor in Venezuela in the early 1800s to be used for its medicinal properties, Angostura bitters are made with a top-secret blend of spices. They've been turning up in cocktails for the past two hundred years and give a warming spice element to many classic drinks.

PEYCHAUD'S Just as popular and nearly as old as Angostura, Peychaud's bitters are lighter and have a little more sweetness. They were created in New Orleans and play a role in many drinks from that cocktail-laden city.

ORANGE Orange bitters give drinks a great kick of citrus without adding sweetness. Look for Regans' or Angostura Orange.

SYRUPS

Essential for adding sweetness to mixed drinks, syrups are the easiest way to get sugar into a cocktail. These eight common syrups turn up consistently, and can be easily made from scratch (recipes start on page 332). Syrups are also an important vehicle for flavor; in addition to the suggestions here, other herbs or spices can be used to infuse a simple syrup.

SIMPLE AND RICH SIMPLE SYRUPS The majority of recipes call for simple syrup, made in a ratio of 1:1 sugar:water, or rich simple syrup, which is 2:1 sugar:water and contributes additional sweetness and texture to a drink due to its viscosity. Either of these can be made with a specific sugar such as Demerara or cane.

HONEY SYRUP Honey is a more flavorful alternative to basic white sugar and can give complexity to simple sours, as in the classic grapefruit and whiskey drink the Brown Derby (page 63).

GINGER SYRUP Fresh ginger syrup adds sweetness along with a nice warming kick to cocktails and, in a pinch, can be used with soda water as a sort of impromptu ginger beer.

CINNAMON SYRUP Simple syrup infused with cinnamon turns up in a good number of tiki cocktails, including the Zombie's "Don's Mix" (page 200), but it also makes appearances in warming drinks, particularly with apple cider.

GRENADINE Made with pomegranate syrup and, thanks to the accessibility of pomegranate juice these days, grenadine is easy to make at home. There are also a number of great bottled versions featuring natural ingredients and eschewing the red dye so common to Shirley Temples.

ORGEAT This almond-based syrup flavored with orange flower water is used in many classic tiki drinks like the Mai Tai (page 113) and the Scorpion Bowl (page 170). Now, a handful of artisan producers are making great bottled versions—even using other nuts—which means there's little reason to mess with DIY.

FALERNUM Made from lime zest, cloves, sugar, ginger, and almonds, this liqueur most likely originated in Barbados in the nineteenth century, and is used as a sweetener in many tiki drinks.

techniques

SUFFICE TO SAY, BARTENDERS ARE an opinionated lot.
But there are a couple baseline principles of mixology that even the
most renegade can agree on: First, to put a drink together, add the
less expensive spirits to the mixing glass or tin first, and the pricier
spirits last. This way, if you make a mistake while measuring you're
less likely to waste pricier ingredients. Second, spirit-forward drinks
ought to be stirred, and drinks with fruit juice should be shaken.
Beyond that, drinks can either be shaken or built in the glass they'll
be served in.

SHAKING

Add the ingredients to a cocktail tin with the base spirit last, fill
with ice, and firmly cover with the smaller mixing tin, tapping it
down with a bump of your fist. With your dominant hand firmly
atop the top tin and the other hand firmly on the bottom of the base
tin, vigorously shake the drink for about 15 seconds, until both tins
are very cold. To open the shakers, give the top tin a good whack
with the heel of your palm to loosen it and remove.

Some recipes call for a "dry shake"—shaking without ice. A dry
shake is used to get some air into the drink, especially important
when using egg whites. To dry shake, fill a shaker with all the
prescribed liquid ingredients, but don't add ice. Shake for about
15 seconds to blend.

STIRRING

Add your ingredients to a mixing glass and fill with ice. Using a
long barspoon held between your thumb and your first two fingers,
gracefully stir the drink, disturbing the ice as little as possible, for

15 to 20 seconds. This action is best achieved by fluidly twirling the back part of the spoon around the bottom inside perimeter of the glass to make sure all of the ingredients are incorporated. You're not looking to crush up the ice, just to achieve a nice, even dilution.

STRAINING

There are a few different types of strainers (see page 25), but they all serve a similar purpose: keeping big chunks of ice or fruit or herbs out of your drink. The Hawthorne strainer is best used with a mixing tin because its spring fits nicely into the interior of the tin, whereas a julep strainer works especially well with a mixing glass.

When a perfectly crystal-clear drink is desired (sans ice shards or bits of citrus), a recipe might call for double straining. To double strain, fit the Hawthorne strainer into the mouth of your mixing tin and hold a fine-mesh strainer over your serving glass with your free hand. Pour the mixed drink through both strainers into the glass.

SWIZZLING

Swizzling ensures that in drinks made with crushed or pebble ice, the ingredients are evenly distributed throughout the glass and fully chilled. Fill the glass with crushed ice, pour in the drink, and then carefully push your barspoon or swizzle stick all the way to the bottom of the drink. Holding the handle between both palms, rub your hands together to rotate the stick or spoon, while pulling it up and down through the ice.

tools

IN THE FACE OF THE mountain of cocktail utensils that have hit the market in the past five years, a less-is-more policy will both keep you sane and ensure you're adequately provisioned for just about any technique. After all, who has that many drawers? Cocktail Kingdom (cocktailkingdom.com) is an excellent source for tools, but most of the following items are available in any good kitchen shop.

Y-SHAPED PEELER

This horizontal vegetable peeler is crucial to making long, perfectly shaped citrus peels and coins for garnishes.

JIGGERS

Eyeballing pours is risky business; even the most experienced bartenders tend to measure out their ingredients to ensure a drink has proper ratios and to cut back on waste. While it's perfectly acceptable to measure out drink ingredients in a measuring cup, a double-sided jigger won't cost much more than a couple of dollars. Invest in one that measures ½ ounce and ¾ ounce, and another that measures 1 ounce and 2 ounces.

SHAKERS

The three-piece shaker (complete with lid and built-in strainer) we're so used to seeing on home bars is rarely used by professional bartenders. Instead, they favor the Boston shaker, a two-tin setup with one smaller tin that fits into a larger tin. Pour your ingredients into the smaller one and cap it with the larger.

MIXING GLASS

If a recipe calls for stirring, you can use just about any vessel, really—a mixing tin, a pint glass—but with all the extraordinarily gorgeous mixing glasses available right now, it's worth putting one on your wish list.

BARSPOON

Will any old spoon work? Sure. But a true, long-handled barspoon will always be able to reach the bottom of your mixing vessel, which is crucial to fully incorporating a drink. A barspoon is also occasionally used as a unit of measurement for small amounts of liquid, and is useful in floating wine or spirits atop a drink.

MUDDLER

This is a wooden baton used for mashing up fruit or pressing herb oils into sugar, as in a Mojito (page 131) or Mint Julep (page 128).

SWIZZLE STICK

A stick with prongs or a paddle at the end, used to stir drinks with crushed ice. Swizzle sticks are traditionally made from a branch from the Caribbean swizzle tree.

STRAINERS

HAWTHORNE Patented in the late nineteenth century, this flat, perforated strainer fits superbly into the mouth of a mixing tin, spring side down.

JULEP Essentially a wide, slotted metal spoon, the julep strainer is best for drinks made in a mixing glass.

FINE-MESH STRAINER This is also known as a tea strainer and is typically used in conjunction with a Hawthorne strainer to "double strain" a drink (like the Florodora, page 85) to remove even fine sediment.

glassware

A DRINK'S VESSEL IS AT least as important as its ingredients, so be sure to use the proper glassware when making cocktails. Start your collection with the essentials—a rocks glass, a coupe or cocktail glass, and a Collins glass—and build from there. And unless your drink is served over ice, make sure you chill the glass before using.

COUPE OR COCKTAIL GLASS

These classic short-stemmed, wide-bowled beauties are used for cocktails, both shaken and stirred, served without ice: anything from a daiquiri to a Boulevardier to a Champagne cocktail.

COLLINS/HIGHBALL/DOUBLE OLD-FASHIONED

Collins glasses (which range in size from 10 ounces to 14 ounces) tend to be a bit narrower and taller than the highball, but they can largely be used interchangeably for long drinks over ice. The double old-fashioned holds the same size drink, but is shorter, with a wide mouth. Use any of these for a fizz, Collins, swizzle, beer cocktail, or highball.

ROCKS OR OLD-FASHIONED

These wide, squat glasses are used for short drinks—both shaken and stirred—that are served over ice. Drinks served in a rocks glass are potent and spirit-forward, and evolve as they dilute. This size glass is also best for single spirits served on the rocks. Use for sours, a Negroni, or an Old-Fashioned.

FLUTE

While the wine world has largely turned its back on flutes, the bar world still appreciates a nice flute for the beads of bubbles the shape creates. Try a flute in place of a coupe for a Champagne cocktail, or Death in the Afternoon (page 82).

SNIFTER

A snifter is designed to focus the aromatics of whatever's in the glass and get them right to your nose, which is why it's a favorite of brandy and cognac drinkers. It can also be used for both spirituous, stirred cocktails and drinks served over crushed ice.

TIKI MUGS

The playful side of tiki drinks extends to the glassware. If you have any interest in this genre of cocktails, stay on the lookout for parrot glasses, skull mugs, and large-format scorpion bowls at yard sales and vintage shops.

JULEP CUP OR TIN

This classic vessel is good for any cocktails made with crushed ice, including its namesake Julep.

MOSCOW MULE MUGS

Since the 1940s, the Moscow Mule mug, like its julep tin cousin, has been intended for one drink alone: a super-cold ginger-spicy Moscow Mule. But don't let that stop you from repurposing it for any other kind of buck.

garnishes

MUCH MORE THAN JUST THE proverbial "cherry on top"—that is, something extra—garnishes help tie the flavors of a drink together. In some cases, they can even be responsible for contributing an essential element that didn't make it into the ingredients themselves. In other words, don't skip the cherry!

CITRUS PEELS

Whether long or round, expressed over a drink or even flamed, citrus peels add their flavor to a drink without additional sweetness.

To flame an orange peel, cut a silver dollar-size piece of peel and hold it, cut side up, a couple of inches above the surface of the drink. Light a match and hold it just beneath, but not touching, the peel. Squeeze the peel, releasing oil that will ignite in a flash of flame.

CITRUS WHEELS, SLICES, AND WEDGES

These hang attractively off the edge of a glass, and can add the flavor of their juice to a drink.

CHERRIES

Though bright red cherries hold a nostalgic allure, a true maraschino cherry such as those produced by Luxardo will contribute a much more complex flavor.

CUCUMBER

In spears or slices, cucumber is an excellent garnish for any drink with a vegetal or herbal flavor.

MINT

If mint appears in a drink's ingredients, it's a sure bet as a garnish.

BERRIES

Most often used to garnish drinks that have berries in the ingredients, these are best saved for when they're in season and at their peak.

PINEAPPLE

Pineapple rounds lend a festive look to a punchbowl, and are a natural complement to tiki drinks.

UMBRELLA

A common companion to tropical drinks, nothing says whimsy like a paper umbrella.

CINNAMON STICK

A flaming cinnamon stick is a suitably flamboyant tiki garnish, and a good match for many drinks featuring spicy flavors, rum, or whiskey.

SALTS AND SUGARS

Use salts, sugars, chile powder, or other spice mixes to "rim" a glass before using it to serve a drink. Pour your seasoning onto a small plate, then run a lemon or lime wedge around the rim of the glass. Invert the glass into the seasoning and then turn it upright.

BITTERS

As a garnish, bitters are especially striking on the frothy white tops of drinks made with egg.

classic
RECIPES

ABSINTHE FRAPPÉ

 | **SERVES 1**

"At the first cold sip on your fevered lip, you determine to live through the day." So went the ode "Absinthe Frappé" from the 1904 musical *It Happened in Nordland*. This drink hails from a time when absinthe was a very popular aperitif (pre-1912 ban) and an acceptable morning pick-me-up. Simple, icy, and strong, the frappé is a less fussy alternative to the pomp and circumstance of traditional absinthe service.

1 OUNCE ABSINTHE	¼–½ OUNCE SIMPLE SYRUP (PAGE 332)	1–2 OUNCES CHILLED WATER

Add all ingredients to a cocktail shaker. Add ice and shake until chilled. Pour into a rocks or Collins glass over crushed or pebble ice. Top with additional ice.

ADONIS

 | **SERVES 1** |

A canonical nineteenth-century sherry aperitif, the Adonis was named after the 1884 Broadway burlesque show of the same name, which is often credited as the first-ever Broadway musical. While the production enjoyed its popularity, the Waldorf Astoria hotel created a cocktail in its honor; its brawny base of fino sherry, combined with orange bitters and sweet vermouth, sets it apart from its cousin, the leaner, drier Bamboo (page 45).

2 OUNCES FINO SHERRY	2 DASHES ORANGE BITTERS, PREFERABLY REGANS'	**GARNISH** ORANGE PEEL
1 OUNCE SWEET VERMOUTH		

Add all ingredients to a mixing glass. Add ice and stir until chilled. Strain into a chilled coupe or cocktail glass. Garnish with an orange peel.

AIRMAIL

 | **SERVES 1** |

The first attempt at modern airmail, though not fully official on account of the plane breaking down, was documented in 1911. Fred Wiseman traveled in a plane he built himself from Petaluma, California, to Santa Rosa, California, with exactly three pieces of correspondence. The first instance of the Airmail cocktail was documented in *Esquire* magazine's 1949 edition of *Handbook for Hosts*. It's not certain why the drink is named for the modern delivery method, but it can be said that the Airmail is quite transportive, like a Caribbean version of a French 75 (page 86).

1½ OUNCES GOLD RUM, PREFERABLY APPLETON OR EL DORADO	¾ OUNCE LIME JUICE	CHAMPAGNE (OR ANY DRY SPARKLING WINE), TO TOP
	SCANT ¾ OUNCE HONEY SYRUP (PAGE 332)	**GARNISH** LIME OR ORANGE PEEL

Add rum, lime juice, and honey syrup to a cocktail shaker. Add ice and shake until chilled. Strain over ice into a Collins glass. Top with Champagne and add a straw. Garnish with a lime or orange peel.

AMERICANO

 | **SERVES 1** |

Don't let the name fool you: the Americano's heritage is most certainly Italian. Born from the Milano-Torino, a nineteenth-century drink made from equal parts Campari (from Milan) and sweet vermouth (from Torino) poured over ice, the Americano is topped up with soda water and garnished with an orange half wheel. Apparently, it was created for lightweight American tourists seeking *la dolce vita* while visiting Italy during Prohibition. Though its boozier cousin, the Negroni (page 135), may have more clout in today's cocktail world, the Americano isn't far behind.

1½ OUNCES CAMPARI	SODA WATER, TO TOP	**GARNISH** ORANGE SLICE
1½ OUNCES SWEET VERMOUTH		

Add Campari and sweet vermouth to a Collins or rocks glass. Add ice and top with soda. Garnish with an orange slice.

APEROL SPRITZ

 | **SERVES 1** |

The spritz construct of sparkling wine, bitter liqueur, and bubbly water is incredibly versatile. But Aperol, the sunset-colored Italian bitter liqueur from Padua, is the classic, providing the lightly sweet base for this afternoon cooler.

1 OUNCE APEROL	2 OUNCES SPARKLING WINE, PREFERABLY DRY PROSECCO	1 OUNCE SODA WATER
		GARNISH ORANGE OR LEMON SLICE (OR BOTH)

Add Aperol, sparkling wine, and soda water to a Collins or wineglass. Add ice and stir gently. Garnish with an orange or lemon slice.

AVIATION

 **SERVES 1**

The comings and goings of classic drinks ride on the availability of ingredients as much as on the wings of fashion. After its 1916 debut in Hugo Ensslin's *Recipes for Mixed Drinks*, this pale violet concoction was lost for almost half a century: first, the cocktail bible of the era, the *Savoy Cocktail Book*, inexplicably dropped the recipe in the 1930s. Then, crème de violette, its hallmark ingredient, was discontinued altogether in the 1960s. In 2007, however, Rothman & Winter re-created the liqueur, making the original Aviation recipe possible again, to the delight of a new generation of bartenders who have since championed this previously forgotten drink.

2 OUNCES GIN

¼ OUNCE MARASCHINO LIQUEUR, PREFERABLY LUXARDO

¼ OUNCE CRÈME DE VIOLETTE, PREFERABLY ROTHMAN & WINTER

½ OUNCE LEMON JUICE

GARNISH BRANDIED CHERRY, PREFERABLY LUXARDO

Add all ingredients to a cocktail shaker. Fill shaker with ice and shake until chilled. Strain into a chilled coupe or cocktail glass. Garnish with a brandied cherry.

NOTE The Aviation can be a tricky cocktail to balance depending on the type of gin, quality of citrus, and sweetness of the crème de violette. For the best results, use a mild, full-bodied gin like Plymouth.

BAMBOO

 | **SERVES 1** |

Of the stirred aperitif drinks of the nineteenth century that involve sherry, two are riffed on again and again, and their names offer clues to their respective styles: the Bamboo is lean and tough, and the brawnier Adonis (page 34), a sort of classical beefcake. Both were conceived around the same time but in different countries. The Bamboo was one of Japan's original cocktails, created by Louis Eppinger, a German bartender (and contemporary of Jerry Thomas) at the Grand Hotel in Yokohama.

1½ OUNCES FINO SHERRY	1 TEASPOON RICH SIMPLE SYRUP (PAGE 332)	2 DASHES ORANGE BITTERS
1½ OUNCES DRY VERMOUTH	2 DASHES ANGOSTURA BITTERS	**GARNISH** LEMON TWIST

Add all ingredients to a mixing glass. Add ice and stir until chilled. Strain into a chilled coupe or cocktail glass. Garnish with a lemon twist.

BEE'S KNEES

 | **SERVES 1** | ⊛

This Roaring Twenties twist on the Gin Sour came into being around the same time flappers like Josephine Baker were doing the Charleston, and darling phrases such as "the cat's whiskers" and "the bee's knees" were contemporary ways of saying "awesome." This simple, refreshing drink is just that. During Prohibition in the United States, honey and lemon juice were smart foils for questionable bootlegged spirits—in this case, gin—that needed masking in the flavor department; today, the flavors are still a great match for any number of artisan gins.

1½ OUNCES GIN	¾ OUNCE HONEY SYRUP (PAGE 332)	**GARNISH** LEMON WHEEL
¾ OUNCE LEMON JUICE		

Add all ingredients to a cocktail shaker. Add ice and shake until chilled. Strain into a chilled coupe or cocktail glass. Garnish with a lemon wheel.

BICICLETTA

 SERVES 1

According to a popular Italian legend, the Bicicletta—"bicycle" in Italian—was named after the elderly men who swerved all over the road while riding home after a few afternoon drinks at the café. In traditional aperitivo style, the cocktail mixes two of Italy's favorite early evening refreshments. Campari adds delightfully bitter complexity to dry Italian white wine, while a splash of soda water turns the combination into a refreshing spritz.

| 1–2 OUNCES CAMPARI | SODA WATER, TO TOP | **GARNISH** |
| 3 OUNCES DRY ITALIAN WHITE WINE | | ORANGE OR LEMON WHEEL |

Add Campari and white wine to a wineglass. Add ice and top with soda. Stir gently and garnish with an orange or lemon wheel.

BIJOU

 **SERVES 1**

This improbable cocktail—a blend of gin, sweet vermouth, and Chartreuse—was invented in the United States in the late nineteenth century. The invention of the drink is commonly attributed to bartender Harry Johnson, who included the recipe in his 1900s tome *The Bartender's Manual*. Its name, which means "jewel" in French, is said to have been inspired by the gem-colored alcohols combined in the recipe. The original formula calls for either a cherry or an olive for a garnish, but history has come down on the correct side of this debate: today's version uses a cherry.

1 OUNCE GIN	¾ OUNCE GREEN CHARTREUSE	**GARNISH** BRANDIED CHERRY, PREFERABLY LUXARDO
1 OUNCE SWEET VERMOUTH	1 DASH ORANGE BITTERS	

Add all ingredients to a mixing glass. Add ice and stir well. Strain into a chilled coupe or cocktail glass. Garnish with a brandied cherry.

BLACK VELVET

 | **SERVES 1**

A fancy man's Black and Tan, this unlikely mourning drink is said to have originated at the Brooks's Club on St. James's Street in London on the occasion of the death of Queen Victoria's husband, Prince Albert, in 1861. The gentleman's club, a brotherhood of the city's most distinguished lords, barons, and dukes, acknowledged the prince's passing the only way they knew how: by having a drink. Apparently, Champagne did not seem appropriate, so it can be surmised that a dark beer was somber enough to foil the celebratory implication of bubbles.

3 OUNCES GUINNESS	3 OUNCES CHAMPAGNE (NO SUBSTITUTE!)

Add Guinness to a coupe, a flute, or a Collins glass. Top gently with Champagne.

BLOOD AND SAND

 | **SERVES 1**

The dramatic title of this cocktail is thought to be a nod to Rudolf Valentino's 1922 silent film of the same name (which was itself an adaption of a 1909 Spanish novel by Vicente Blasco Ibáñez) about the rise and fall of a bullfighter. This rather unexpected concoction of equal parts Scotch, sweet vermouth, cherry liqueur, and orange juice, shaken and strained, makes for one of the rare classic cocktails that calls for Scotch as a base. Be sure to use fresh-squeezed orange juice here; it gives the right jab of acidity in the context of two sweet liqueurs.

---

1 OUNCE SCOTCH, PREFERABLY BLENDED

1 OUNCE CHERRY LIQUEUR, PREFERABLY CHERRY HEERING

1 OUNCE SWEET VERMOUTH

1 OUNCE ORANGE JUICE

Add all ingredients to a cocktail shaker. Add ice and shake. Strain into a chilled coupe or cocktail glass.

NOTE Not all cherry liqueurs are created equal; your best bet for this drink is the Danish liqueur Cheery Heering for its depth of flavor and balanced sweetness.

BLOODY MARY

 | **SERVES 1** |

Before there was brunch, there was the Bloody Mary. The drink boasts numerous mythologies, ranging from a start as a warm, nonalcoholic beverage loaded with raw oysters to one named in honor of a barmaid from Chicago's Buckets of Blood. Whatever the case, the Bloody Mary eventually became a staple of Manhattan's King Cole Bar at the St. Regis, where it was downed by New York's toniest barflies. Swapping out vodka for alternate spirits creates the Red Snapper (gin), Bloody Maria (tequila), and Bloody Derby (bourbon), or go the way of the Michelada (page 124) and lighten the whole thing up with a fizzy beer.

---

2 OUNCES VODKA

4 OUNCES
TOMATO JUICE

½ OUNCE
LEMON JUICE

½ TEASPOON
WORCESTERSHIRE

2-4 DASHES HOT SAUCE

SALT AND PEPPER
TO TASTE

GARNISH
CELERY STALK OR
LIME WEDGE

Add all ingredients to a mixing tin and add ice. Roll back and forth between mixing tins and strain into an ice-filled Collins or highball glass. Garnish with a celery stick, lime wedge, crispy bacon, shrimp, or any other outrageous items you can come up with.

BOULEVARDIER

 | **SERVES 1** |

A true man-about-town and boulevardier in the literal sense of the word, Erskine Gwynne was an individual of epic reputation throughout Paris in the 1920s. In fact, he even ran a magazine called *Boulevardier* for American ex-pats living in the city. Mention of this literary-influenced cocktail appears in the 1927 book *Barflies and Cocktails* by Harry MacElhone (owner of Harry's New York Bar in Paris), which credits Gwynne as the drink's creator. Depending on the audience, the Boulevardier can be seen as a bittersweet Manhattan variation or a whiskey Negroni. The beauty of the Boulevardier is its adaptability to both bitter and sweet, so depending on the base spirit, an array of amari and vermouth can be used to play to the chosen whiskey's strengths.

1½ OUNCES
BOURBON OR RYE

1 OUNCE CAMPARI

1 OUNCE SWEET
VERMOUTH

GARNISH
ORANGE PEEL

Add all ingredients to a mixing glass. Add ice and stir until chilled. Strain over ice into a rocks glass. (Or, strain into a chilled coupe or cocktail glass.) Garnish with an orange peel.

BROOKLYN

 | **SERVES 1**

Everyone knows that Manhattan might be the go-to for luxury and fashion, but if you want something that's more cutting edge you have to go to Brooklyn. The same is true of the borough-designated cocktails. Although the Prohibition-era Brooklyn shares a similar flavor profile and composition to a Manhattan (page 114), the more esoteric additions of both Amer Picon (largely unavailable in the States) and maraschino liqueur have kept it from taking its place as a top-tier classic drink. But just as Brooklyn has been stealing the spotlight in terms of New York City bars of late, an enthusiasm for DIY Amer Picon has inspired a rise in popularity for the Brooklyn cocktail. If Amer Picon is unavailable, Amaro CioCiaro will work just fine.

| 2 OUNCES RYE | ¼ OUNCE | ¼ OUNCE |
| 1/2 OUNCE DRY VERMOUTH | MARASCHINO LIQUEUR | AMER PICON |

Add all ingredients to a mixing glass. Add ice and stir until chilled. Strain into a coupe.

BROWN DERBY

 | **SERVES 1** |

Born on the posh Sunset Boulevard in West Hollywood, Los Angeles, the Brown Derby is a vestige of 1930s glitz and glamour. A heady mix of bourbon, grapefruit, and honey, it was created at the Vendôme Club—one of the first celebrity-driven restaurants to appear on the Sunset Strip—which was then owned by *Hollywood Reporter* founder and playboy Billy Wilkerson. The drink was named in honor of a nearby restaurant, the Brown Derby (best known as the birthplace of the Cobb salad), which was actually built in the shape of a rotund derby hat.

1½ OUNCES BOURBON	¾ OUNCE GRAPEFRUIT JUICE	**GARNISH** GRAPEFRUIT PEEL
	¾ OUNCE HONEY SYRUP (PAGE 332)	

Add all ingredients to a cocktail shaker. Add ice and shake until chilled. Strain into a chilled coupe. Garnish with a grapefruit peel.

CAIPIRINHA

 | **SERVES 1** |

A relative of the Daiquiri (page 74), this strong sweet-sour drink calls for cachaça, a Brazilian take on rum that's distilled from fermented sugarcane juice. The Caipirinha, truly Brazil's national drink, is a combination of lime juice, sugar, and cachaça, and it was thought to have originated to mask the taste of the crudely produced spirit. Until recently, cachaça was widely considered a peasants' spirit, but as production techniques have improved, so has the cocktail.

1 LIME, QUARTERED

2 TEASPOONS SUGAR

2 OUNCES CACHAÇA

GARNISH
LIME WHEEL

To a rocks glass, add lime wedges and sugar and muddle until well juiced. Add cachaça and ice. Stir to mix and garnish with a lime wheel.

CHAMPAGNE COCKTAIL

 **SERVES 1**

Swap Champagne for whiskey in the Old-Fashioned template, and you'll get this pedigreed cocktail, which was first mentioned in Jerry Thomas's 1862 *How to Mix Drinks*. Its low-alcohol and bubbly constitution make this recipe a good candidate for day drinking. The question as to whether you pony up for the real stuff or choose a down-market sparkling wine depends largely on your opinion of the sanctity of Champagne.

1 SUGAR CUBE OR 1 BARSPOON SUGAR	3 DASHES ANGOSTURA BITTERS	**GARNISH** LONG, CURLY LEMON PEEL
	CHAMPAGNE, TO TOP	

Add the sugar cube or sugar to a flute. Add Angostura bitters to soak the sugar. Slowly top up with Champagne. Garnish with a long, curly lemon peel.

NOTE A dry sparkling wine like Crémant de Bourgogne is best if you don't have Champagne on hand. Also, the type of bitters used can dramatically alter the drink. While Angostura is classic, playing around is encouraged. Brad Thomas Parsons, author of *Bitters*, adds an element of citrus, employing yuzu or Meyer lemon bitters in combination with a dot of Angostura to maintain "that pretty amber hue."

CHARLES DICKENS'S PUNCH

 | **SERVES 10** |

There are few things more Dickensian than a bowl of punch. A great lover of drink, Dickens wove spirits into his writing repeatedly and even conceived of his own punch: this cheek-warming mix of Cognac, rum, citrus, and sugar that is "cooked" by setting it on fire.

¾ CUP SUGAR, PREFERABLY DEMERARA	2 CUPS RUM, PREFERABLY SMITH & CROSS	5 CUPS BLACK TEA (OR HOT WATER)
3 LEMONS, PEELED AND JUICE RESERVED	1¼ CUPS COGNAC, PREFERABLY COURVOISIER VSOP	**GARNISH** LEMON AND ORANGE SLICES, FRESHLY GRATED NUTMEG

To an enameled cast-iron pot or heatproof bowl, add sugar and lemon peels. Muddle peels and sugar together to release citrus oils.

Add rum and Cognac to the sugar. Light a match, and, using a heatproof spoon, pick up a spoonful of the spirit mix. Carefully bring the match to the spoon to light, then bring the lit spoon back to the bowl. Let the spirits burn for about 3 minutes. The fire will melt the sugar and extract the oil from the lemon peels.

Extinguish the fire by covering it with a heatproof pan. Skim off lemon peels. Squeeze in the lemon juice, and add hot tea.

Ladle into glasses over ice. Garnish with citrus slices and grated nutmeg.

CLOVER CLUB

 | **SERVES 1** |

The Bellevue-Stratford in Philadelphia was *the* fashionable, see-and-be-seen hotel of the late 1800s. Like the Friars Club or the Algonquin Round Table of its era, the establishment hosted an all-male salon of lawyers and writers—the Clover Club—until World War I. The cocktail didn't appear until later in the club's history and it eventually fell out of fashion, most likely due to its perilous inclusion of egg white and feminine associations with raspberries. But like many of the pre-Prohibition stalwarts, the drink was rediscovered as part of the classic arsenal, and made immortal by Julie Reiner at her Brooklyn bar, Clover Club.

3–4 RASPBERRIES

SCANT ½ OUNCE
SIMPLE SYRUP
(PAGE 332)

1½ OUNCES GIN,
PREFERABLY
PLYMOUTH

½ OUNCE DRY
VERMOUTH,
PREFERABLY DOLIN

½ OUNCE LEMON
JUICE

¼ OUNCE EGG WHITE

Add raspberries to a cocktail shaker and muddle along with simple syrup. Add remaining ingredients and dry shake. Add ice and shake again until chilled. Double strain into a chilled coupe or cocktail glass. Garnish with a skewered raspberry.

CORPSE REVIVER NO. 2

 | **SERVES 1** |

Of the entire gruesomely named family of pre-Prohibition era drinks thought to be devoted to rousing oneself in the morning, version No. 2 remains the best known. A lighter-spirited relation to the cognac-heavy Sidecar (page 177), with gin and Lillet in equal proportions to Cointreau, this drink finishes fresh and citrusy, with a hint of herbal complexity from the absinthe. Such a cocktail is a reasonable choice for eye-opening activities if you heed the warning offered in the 1930 *Savoy Cocktail Book*: "Four of these taken in swift succession will un-revive the corpse again."

1 DASH ABSINTHE	1 OUNCE COINTREAU	**GARNISH** LEMON PEEL
1 OUNCE GIN	1 OUNCE LILLET BLANC	
	1 OUNCE LEMON JUICE	

To a chilled coupe or cocktail glass, add a dash of absinthe. Roll around to coat and discard excess. Add remaining ingredients to a cocktail shaker. Add ice and shake until chilled. Strain into the prepared glass. Garnish with a lemon peel.

DAIQUIRI

 **SERVES 1**

Thanks to spring break destinations like Fort Lauderdale and Key West, the word *daiquiri* carries the connotation of whirring machines spinning electric-colored drinks. But the true recipe is a minimalist classic. Although a U.S. engineer living in Cuba during the Spanish-American War usually gets credit for the recipe, it's more likely that Cubans had been drinking something similar for some time. Famously associated with author Ernest Hemingway and the jet-set glamour of pre-embargo Cuba in the 1930s, the Daiquiri rose in popularity in the United States during World War II as Caribbean rum became much easier to procure than foreign whiskey. These days, it's become an international calling card for bartenders looking to test each other's chops. It's a drink that can easily be out of whack if it doesn't have a proper balance of rum, sugar, and citrus, but it can also be brilliantly transformed with even the smallest tweak.

---

2 OUNCES LIGHT RUM

1 OUNCE LIME JUICE

¾ OUNCE SIMPLE
SYRUP (PAGE 332)

GARNISH
LIME WHEEL

Add all ingredients to a cocktail shaker. Add ice and shake until chilled. Strain into a chilled coupe or cocktail glass. Garnish with a lime wheel.

DANIEL WEBSTER'S PUNCH

 | **SERVES 10**

In his book *Punch*, David Wondrich attributes the myriad versions of this recipe to the fact that asking for a glass of Webster's Punch was the nineteenth-century version of "stump the bartender." No one really knew which version the famed Massachusetts senator actually preferred, so riffs abound. The original version of this recipe, adapted by Wondrich, comes from the *Steward & Barkeeper's Manual* (1869).

½ CUP SUGAR

3 LEMONS, PEELED AND JUICE RESERVED

2 CUPS BLACK TEA

¾ CUP COGNAC

¾ CUP DRY OLOROSO SHERRY

¾ CUP JAMAICAN RUM

1½ CUPS BORDEAUX, OR ANY FULL-BODIED RED WINE

CHAMPAGNE, TO TOP

GARNISH
FRUIT-EMBELLISHED ICE RING (SEE NOTE)

In a large bowl, combine sugar and lemon peels, then lightly muddle and let sit for 20 minutes. Then, add tea, lemon juice, Cognac, sherry, rum, and red wine and stir to combine. Strain out lemon peels and refrigerate for about 30 minutes. Fifteen minutes before serving, add ice ring. Ladle into cups and lightly top each portion with Champagne.

NOTE To make an ice ring, fill a Bundt pan halfway with water. Evenly place 5 strawberry halves, 5 pineapple slices, and 10 mint leaves in the water, then freeze overnight.

DARK 'N' STORMY

 **SERVES 1**

This simple mix of dark rum and spicy ginger beer, served long over ice, has roots in colonial Bermuda, where England's Royal Navy opened a ginger beer plant in the late nineteenth century. The drink was traditionally made with a dark, heavy Demerara-style rum, which was part of the sailors' daily rations. Today, most bartenders perk up the drink with a welcome dose of lime juice. Be aware that a number of years ago, Gosling Brothers bought the trademark to the Dark 'n' Stormy name and recipe, so Gosling's Black Seal rum is the official rum of record for this drink.

2 OUNCES DARK OR
BLACKSTRAP RUM

1 OUNCE LIME JUICE

4 OUNCES DRY, SPICY
GINGER BEER

GARNISH
LIME WHEEL

Add rum and lime juice to a Collins glass. Add ice and top with ginger beer. Garnish with a lime wheel.

DE LA LOUISIANE

 **SERVES 1**

This deep, boozy number goes by other names, including La Louisiane and Cocktail à la Louisiane. As its French-inflected name hints, it's a New Orleans creation. In his authoritative 1937 book, *Famous New Orleans Drinks and How to Mix 'Em*, Stanley Clisby Arthur notes that it was Restaurant La Louisiane's house cocktail, where it presumably paired well with the rich, sometimes fiery Creole cuisine.

2 OUNCES RYE, PREFERABLY DICKEL

¾ OUNCE BÉNÉDICTINE

½ OUNCE SWEET VERMOUTH, PREFERABLY CARPANO ANTICA

3 DASHES ABSINTHE

3 DASHES PEYCHAUD'S BITTERS

GARNISH
BRANDIED CHERRY, PREFERABLY LUXARDO

Add all ingredients to a mixing glass. Add ice and stir until chilled. Strain into a chilled cocktail glass or coupe. Garnish with a brandied cherry.

DEATH IN THE AFTERNOON

 | **SERVES 1**

Bizarrely, Ernest Hemingway extended the gravitas of *Death in the Afternoon*, the title of his 1932 novel about the denouement of bullfighting in Spain, to this minimalist cocktail that's nothing more than Champagne with a shot of absinthe. The recipe ran in a celebrity drinks book in 1932. The seriousness with which Hemingway approached his cocktail was evidenced by his recipe instructions: to drink three to five of these at a time. Undoubtedly, the diabetic Hemingway would have made his cocktail without sugar, but the pointed drink is nicely softened with a little bit of sweetness. Add simple syrup to your taste.

¼ – ½ OUNCE ABSINTHE	1 DASH SIMPLE SYRUP (PAGE 332, OPTIONAL)	CHAMPAGNE OR DRY SPARKLING WINE, TO TOP

Add absinthe and simple syrup (if using) to a flute. Slowly top with chilled Champagne or sparkling wine.

FLORODORA

 **SERVES 1**

This pink stunner is an homage to the "Florodora Sextette," six scandalously beautiful young ladies who danced in the 1900 musical *Florodora* at New York's Casino Theatre. Just like the dancers who went on to marry millionaires—as David Wondrich recounts in his book, *Imbibe!*—the Florodora cocktail is unapologetically alluring, a mess of muddled raspberries swirled with lime, gin, and ginger soda. It was most definitely drunk by the well-heeled crowds who sidled up to its likely barroom of origin, at the Waldorf Astoria hotel.

4 RASPBERRIES	1½ OUNCES GIN	**GARNISH**
½ OUNCE SIMPLE SYRUP (PAGE 332)	¾ OUNCE LIME JUICE	ORANGE WHEEL, LIME WHEEL, AND A RASPBERRY
	GINGER ALE, TO TOP	

In a cocktail shaker, muddle raspberries with simple syrup. Add gin, lime juice, and ice and shake until chilled. Double strain into a Collins glass over ice. Top up with ginger ale. Garnish with an orange wheel, lime wheel, and a raspberry.

FRENCH 75

 | **SERVES 1** |

History says that this Champagne cocktail originated at Harry's New York bar in Paris in the early 1900s, but it was co-opted and made legendary shortly thereafter by Arnaud's French 75 bar in New Orleans. The original recipe calls for Cognac combined with Champagne, lemon juice, and sugar, but somewhere along the line, it became fashionable to make the drink with gin instead. But Arnaud's stays the course with Cognac, which gives the cocktail more depth and a little bit of spice, making it a great bubbly drink for the fall and winter. The livelier gin version (a gin sour royale, really) is best in warm weather.

2 OUNCES COGNAC OR GIN	¼ OUNCE SIMPLE SYRUP (PAGE 332)	**GARNISH** LONG, CURLY LEMON PEEL
½ OUNCE LEMON JUICE	3 OUNCES CHAMPAGNE OR DRY SPARKLING WINE	

Add Cognac, lemon juice, and simple syrup to a cocktail shaker. Add ice and shake until chilled. Strain into a coupe or a flute and top with champagne or sparkling wine. Garnish with a long, curly lemon peel.

GARIBALDI

 **SERVES 1**

A classic Garibaldi, named for military general Giuseppe Garibaldi, who's credited with unifying Italy in the mid-1800s, is traditionally a union of equal parts Campari and fresh orange juice, served in a small, tall glass. But this variation on Naren Young's version from New York's Dante, dials back the Campari and focuses on the citrus, using what he calls "fluffy orange juice," a super-aerated juice that he squeezes to order using the bar's high-speed juicer. Obviously, not everyone has a fancy juicer, so just use the freshest OJ you can and shake the drink to further aerate the juice.

1½ OUNCES CAMPARI	4 OUNCES FRESH ORANGE JUICE	**GARNISH** ORANGE WEDGE

Add Campari and orange juice to a cocktail shaker with ice and shake until very cold. Strain over ice into a lowball glass. Garnish with an orange wedge.

GIBSON

 **SERVES 1**

This cocktail is a good example of how powerful a garnish can be. Here, a tiny pearlescent onion transforms a bitters-less martini into an entirely new drink: the Gibson. The usual historical squabbles exist about the drink's origins and namesake (in short: at San Francisco's Bohemian Club in the 1890s for Walter D. K. Gibson, or for illustrator Charles Dana Gibson, among many others), but no one can seem to pinpoint when or why a pickled onion made it into the recipe, as the earliest versions did not call for it. By the mid-twentieth century, though, the Gibson—onion included—appeared to represent a challenge to the martini in terms of cultural cachet.

| 2 OUNCES GIN | 1 OUNCE DRY VERMOUTH | **GARNISH** COCKTAIL ONION (SEE NOTE) |

Add all ingredients to a mixing glass. Add ice and stir until chilled. Strain into a chilled coupe or cocktail glass. Garnish with a cocktail onion.

NOTE For a quick pickled cocktail onion, peel a handful of pearl onions and place in a jar filled with white vinegar and a pinch of sugar. Let infuse for several hours or up to 1 week in the refrigerator.

GIMLET

 | **SERVES 1** |

Leave it up to the Royal Navy to devise a health plan that involved gin. The story goes that the gimlet was created in the mid-nineteenth century to encourage sailors to consume their rations of scurvy-preventing lime juice. The name? Possibly a reference to Thomas Desmond Gimlette, a naval medical officer who served during that era. Essentially a Gin Sour (page 102) with lime juice, the drink went on to become a country-club favorite thanks to its just-off-the-court refreshing side.

2 OUNCES GIN	¾ OUNCE SIMPLE SYRUP (PAGE 332)	**GARNISH**
¾ OUNCE LIME JUICE		LIME WHEEL

Add all ingredients to a cocktail shaker. Add ice and shake until chilled. Strain into a chilled coupe or cocktail glass or over ice into a rocks glass, if you prefer. Garnish with a lime wheel.

NOTE Before fresh juice was standard in cocktails, Rose's Lime Cordial was *the* go-to for gimlets. Although some fundamentalists still insist that a gimlet is not a gimlet without Rose's, no self-respecting bartender would stand for using the artificially flavored sweetener.

GIN AND TONIC

 **SERVES 1**

The humble gin and tonic has a much more storied history than one would think. A founding member of the highball family of cocktails, the drink was initially consumed by members of the British military in the mid-1850s in an effort to stave off malaria while expanding the British empire. It was discovered that the quinine in tonic, made from the bark of the cinchona tree, was a remedy for the disease, and the British predilection for gin found its way into this medicine. While it's perfectly acceptable to stick to the basic formula of a couple ounces of gin served long with tonic water and a nice squeeze of lime, the modern era of cocktails offers up all sorts of gins, artisan tonic waters, and a slew of bartenders who have expanded on the classic.

2 OUNCES GIN	TONIC WATER, TO TOP	**GARNISH** LIME WEDGE

Add gin to a highball glass and fill with ice. Fill the glass with tonic water. Garnish with a lime wedge.

GIN DAISY (OLD AND NEW)

 | **SERVES 1** |

As with many of the classics, there are actually two genres of Gin Daisy, with a historical dividing line somewhere around the turn of the twentieth century. The basic daisy formula, as designed in the 1870s, is more or less a sour kicked up with a few dashes of orange liqueur. Later, the daisy got a makeover: the gin ratio was knocked down, simple syrup was added for texture, and grenadine was swapped in for the orange liqueur. Both renditions are simple, quaffable drinks that deserve more play. Follow this recipe for the true old-school version, or try her fruitier sister, below.

2 OUNCES GIN	¾ OUNCE LEMON JUICE	**GARNISH** LEMON WHEEL
¾ OUNCE ORANGE LIQUEUR	SODA WATER, TO TOP	

Add gin, orange liqueur, and lemon juice to a cocktail shaker. Add ice and shake until chilled. Strain over ice into a rocks or Collins glass and top up with soda water. Garnish with a lemon wheel.

To make the new-school Gin Daisy, add 1½ ounces gin, ½ ounce lemon juice, ¼ ounce grenadine (page 333), and ¼ ounce simple syrup (page 332) to a cocktail shaker. Add ice and shake until chilled. Strain over ice into a Collins or rocks glass and top with soda water. Garnish with an orange slice.

GIN FIZZ

 | **SERVES 1**

The classic nineteenth-century fizz template is one of the most widely adapted in the cocktail canon, but it's the levity of a simple gin version that's made it most famous. The herbal, citrusy character of the base spirit shows well alongside the sweet-sour combo of citrus and simple syrup, all lightened by soda water. Kissing cousin to the Tom Collins (page 189), this fizz recipe leans slightly heavier on the gin for a more assertive kick. Note that the fizz is not served over ice; it's meant to be slurped quickly and efficiently without the addition of extra dilution.

---

2 OUNCES GIN

¾ OUNCE
LEMON JUICE

¾ OUNCE SIMPLE
SYRUP (PAGE 332)

2 DASHES ORANGE
BITTERS

SODA WATER,
TO TOP

Add gin, lemon juice, simple syrup, and orange bitters to a cocktail shaker. Add ice and shake until chilled. Strain into a fizz or highball glass. Top with soda water.

GIN RICKEY

SERVES 1

The Rickey, a variation on the classic fizz, traces its origins to a whiskey-based drink created by Joe Rickey, a lobbyist from Missouri who moved to the nation's capital in the late nineteenth century. Once in Washington, D.C., Rickey became a regular at Shoomaker's Saloon and started many of his days there, ordering what he called his "mornin's mornin'": two ounces of whiskey, long, with soda water over ice. The drink was a hit and soon found nationwide popularity, so much so that Rickey eventually got into the drinks business himself, selling soda water. This version replaces whiskey with gin and adds lime juice, which has arguably become the drink's most famous riff.

2 OUNCES GIN, PREFERABLY LONDON DRY	½ – ¾ OUNCE LIME JUICE	**GARNISH** LIME WHEEL
	SODA WATER, TO TOP	

Add gin and lime juice to a Collins glass. Add ice and top with soda water. Garnish with a lime wheel.

GIN SOUR

 **SERVES 1**

A direct descendant of punch, the basic sour forms the template for a host of modern drinks. First mentions of the sour, made from a base spirit, citrus, sugar, and water and served neat in a small bar glass, can be traced to the mid-nineteenth century. This version strikes a dry and citrusy balance between gin and lemon juice.

2 OUNCES GIN

¾ OUNCE LEMON JUICE

¾ OUNCE SIMPLE SYRUP (PAGE 332)

GARNISH LEMON PEEL

Add all ingredients to a cocktail shaker. Add ice and shake until chilled. Strain into a chilled coupe or cocktail glass. Garnish with a lemon peel.

HEMINGWAY DAIQUIRI

 **SERVES 1**

With his prodigious constitution for drinking (and writing about it), Ernest Hemingway shows up frequently in cocktail mythology, and in none perhaps more famously than in connection to this drink. La Floridita, a Havana bar where the author was a regular in the 1920s, served Hemingway these doctored-up daiquiris, made unique by the addition of maraschino liqueur and notable for the lack of simple syrup (thought to be because Hemingway was diabetic). He could reportedly pack away tens of these at a time, ordering doubles— or what would come to be known as the "Papa Doble" in tribute.

2 OUNCES WHITE RUM	¾ OUNCE LIME JUICE	**GARNISH**
½ OUNCE MARASCHINO LIQUEUR, PREFERABLY LUXARDO	½ OUNCE GRAPEFRUIT JUICE	LIME WHEEL

Add all ingredients to a cocktail shaker. Add ice and shake until chilled. Strain into a chilled coupe or cocktail glass. Garnish with a lime wheel.

IMPROVED WHISKEY COCKTAIL

 | **SERVES 1** |

A little liquorous history helps answer the question the name of this cocktail begs to ask: improved on what? Long before American bartenders had access to European liqueurs, their resources were essentially limited to spirits, sugar, and bitters. A surprising number of drinks, including the old-fashioned, were created from these three simple ingredients. The next wave of "improved" cocktails featured a lemon peel rubbed around the rim of a glass and the addition of a sweet liqueur. The Improved Whiskey Cocktail, the most enduring of them all, serves as a window into a moment in cocktail history when drinks were progressing in complexity.

1 SUGAR CUBE, 1 TEASPOON GRANULATED SUGAR, OR ¼ OUNCE SIMPLE SYRUP (PAGE 332)

1 BARSPOON MARASCHINO LIQUEUR

1 DASH ANGOSTURA BITTERS

1 DASH PEYCHAUD'S BITTERS

1 DASH ABSINTHE

2 OUNCES BOURBON OR RYE

GARNISH
LEMON PEEL

In a rocks glass, muddle sugar cube (or sugar or simple syrup) with maraschino liqueur, both bitters, and absinthe. Add whiskey and stir. Add ice (preferably a large cube) and stir until well chilled. Garnish with a lemon peel.

JUNGLE BIRD

 | **SERVES 1** |

A "simple" tiki cocktail—it contains only five ingredients—the Jungle Bird is rumored to have been created in the late 1970s at the Kuala Lumpur Hilton. The addition of bitter, bracing Campari to a base of Jamaican or blackstrap rum is one more way the Bird stands out from the rest of the tiki canon. The drink has migrated back into the bartenders' repertoires of late, in sync with the modern American palate, which has adopted a hankering for all things Campari. Pineapple and lime smooth any rough edges and add a characteristically tropical vibe to this classic.

1½ OUNCES RUM, JAMAICAN OR BLACKSTRAP

¾ OUNCE CAMPARI

½ OUNCE LIME JUICE

½ OUNCE SIMPLE SYRUP (PAGE 332)

1½ OUNCES PINEAPPLE JUICE

GARNISH
PINEAPPLE WEDGE

Add all ingredients to a cocktail shaker. Add ice and shake until chilled. Strain over ice into a tiki mug or a rocks glass. Garnish with a pineapple wedge.

LAST WORD

 | **SERVES 1** |

Detroit seemingly played a very minor role in contributing to Prohibition-era drinks, but the Last Word exists entirely thanks to the Motor City. Equal parts four ingredients, it was first served at the Detroit Athletic Club, most likely mixed with bathtub gin during America's dark days of temperance. Ted Saucier, author of the 1951 cocktail manual *Bottoms Up!*, attributes the invention to vaudeville monologist Frank Fogarty, whose wit often earned him the last laugh. The cocktail was revived in the early aughts when bartender Murray Stenson, formerly of Seattle's Zig Zag Café, came across the recipe while researching old bar manuals. It quickly became a staple at the Zig Zag and a beloved revival within the cocktail world.

¾ OUNCE GIN	¾ OUNCE LIME JUICE	**GARNISH**
¾ OUNCE GREEN CHARTREUSE	¾ OUNCE MARASCHINO LIQUEUR, PREFERABLY LUXARDO	BRANDIED CHERRY, PREFERABLY LUXARDO

Add all ingredients to a cocktail shaker. Add ice and shake until chilled. Strain into a chilled coupe or cocktail glass. Garnish with a brandied cherry.

MAI TAI

 | **SERVES 1** |

The credit for this iconic 1940s drink—whose name is a nod to the Tahitian word *maita'i*, which means "good"—is usually given to venerable Los Angeles tiki bar Trader Vic's. Buoyed by the rise of tiki culture and some big celebrity endorsements (think Elvis in *Blue Hawaii*), this rum-based drink became cemented in the public imagination as a tropical must-have. But don't look to this drink for kitsch factor alone: when done up right—without orange juice or syrupy prefab mai tai mix—this is one of the greats. This version—a recipe interpreted by modern-day tiki bartender Brian Miller—is based on Trader Vic's 1944 original.

½ OUNCE WHITE RHUM AGRICOLE, PREFERABLY NEISSON L'ESPRIT RHUM

½ OUNCE GOLD RUM, PREFERABLY HAMILTON JAMAICAN GOLD

½ OUNCE AGED RUM, PREFERABLY EL DORADO 15-YEAR

½ OUNCE AGED RUM, PREFERABLY APPLETON 12-YEAR RUM OR PLANTATION JAMAICA 2001

½ OUNCE CLÉMENT CRÉOLE SHRUBB, OR ORANGE CURAÇAO, LIKE PIERRE FERRAND DRY CURAÇAO

1 OUNCE LIME JUICE

¾ OUNCE ORGEAT, PREFERABLY ORGEAT WORKS OR SMALL HAND FOODS

GARNISH
LIME WHEEL, AND A SPRIG OF MINT (OPTIONAL)

Add all ingredients to a cocktail shaker. Add ice and shake until chilled. Strain over crushed ice into a rocks glass. Garnish with a lime wheel and a sprig of mint, if desired.

NOTE Using good orgeat is key to any decent mai tai. Small Hand Foods' version is first-rate.

MANHATTAN

 | **SERVES 1** |

Two cocktails every American knows by name are undoubtedly the crystal-clear martini and its dark and deep ally, the Manhattan. The heady duo rely on a solid spirituous base, amplified by vermouth (dry for the martini, sweet for the Manhattan), and are recognized by their signature garnishes: olives for the former, and a brandied cherry for the latter. Over the course of the twentieth century, the martini largely pulled back on the vermouth, becoming even more bracing, but the Manhattan has remained resolute in its ratio.

2 OUNCES RYE OR BOURBON	2 DASHES ANGOSTURA BITTERS	**GARNISH**
1 OUNCE SWEET VERMOUTH		BRANDIED CHERRIES, PREFERABLY LUXARDO

Add all ingredients to a mixing glass. Add ice and stir well. Strain into a chilled coupe or cocktail glass. Garnish with a brandied cherry or three.

MARGARITA

 | **SERVES 1** |

The true margarita—a blend of tequila, fresh lime juice, orange liqueur, and sugar—is a potent, well-built classic. It was once believed to be a south-of-the-border twist on the popular daisy (a legend bolstered by linguistics: *margarita* is "daisy" in Spanish); over the years, credit for its invention has also been claimed by a Tijuana restaurateur and an Acapulco socialite. In December 1953 it was named *Esquire*'s cocktail of the month, and it has hardly flagged in popularity since. Whatever its original provenance, this version is a sure bet: a hybrid of the old-school and the modern classic Tommy's Margarita that pairs an agave-based sweetener with tequila.

1½ OUNCES
BLANCO TEQUILA

¾ OUNCE ORANGE
LIQUEUR, PREFERABLY
COINTREAU

¾ OUNCE
LIME JUICE

1 TEASPOON
AGAVE NECTAR

GARNISH
SALT FOR RIM
(OPTIONAL) AND
A LIME WHEEL

Prepare a rocks, coupe, or cocktail glass with a salted rim (see page 29), if desired. Add all ingredients to a cocktail shaker. Add ice and shake until chilled. Strain into prepared glass, over ice if desired. Garnish with a lime wheel.

NOTE If you're using an orange liqueur other than Cointreau, adjust the lime juice up according to the liqueur's sweetness.

MARTINEZ

 | **SERVES 1** |

Is the Martinez a predecessor to the martini? This is yet another lineage cocktail historians love to bicker over. One camp is certain that the Martinez is the parent, and the other is sure that the two were contemporaries. Traditionally made with Old Tom Gin (a sweeter style), sweet vermouth, and maraschino liqueur, the drink does skew a bit saccharine when compared with a dry martini. These same historians also debate the origin of the Martinez: some credit a bar in the city of Martinez, California; others say Jerry Thomas made it for a traveler headed there. Either way, the first known published recipe can be found in *The Modern Bartender's Guide*, an 1884 book by O. H. Byron.

---

1 OUNCE GIN

1½ OUNCES SWEET VERMOUTH

1 TEASPOON MARASCHINO LIQUEUR, PREFERABLY LUXARDO

2 DASHES ANGOSTURA BITTERS

GARNISH
ORANGE PEEL

Add all ingredients to a mixing glass. Add ice and stir until chilled. Strain into a chilled coupe or cocktail glass. Garnish with an orange peel.

MARTINI

 | **SERVES 1** |

Considering all of the sleuthing done by cocktail historians, it's remarkable that no one has turned up a solid story for the birth of the martini. Certain facts, however, have been established: the martini postdated the Manhattan and probably evolved from a mix of sweet vermouth and sweet gin as drier versions of those alcohols became popular at the turn of the twentieth century. Over time, the bitters fell out of fashion, as did vermouth, and the ratio of the drink tilted strongly to gin. The cocktail revival has righted some of these wrong turns, but there now exists a world of permutations regarding the ratio of vermouth to gin, garnishing with an olive or a twist, and even, yes, shaken or stirred. For the most authentic version: your choice, your choice, stirred.

---

2 OUNCES GIN

1 OUNCE DRY VERMOUTH, PREFERABLY DOLIN

2 DASHES ORANGE BITTERS

GARNISH LEMON PEEL

Add all ingredients to a mixing glass. Add ice and stir until chilled. Strain into a chilled coupe or cocktail glass. Garnish with an expressed (twisted over top to release the fragrant oils) lemon peel.

NOTE Should you prefer a drier martini, try a 4:1 ratio of gin to vermouth. A dirty martini simply requires a splash of olive juice and the substitution of a good, dry olive (or two) for garnish.

MEXICAN FIRING SQUAD

 | **SERVES 1** |

A discovery of cocktail writer, historian, and wanderlust Charles H. Baker Jr., the Mexican Firing Squad is recorded in his 1939 *The Gentleman's Companion, Volume II: Being an Exotic Drinking Book or Around the World with Jigger, Beaker and Flask*. He'd encountered the Firing Squad at La Cucaracha Bar, a Prohibition-era favorite, in Mexico City, on one of his Latin American journeys. A dry formula, the Firing Squad is almost a Rickey (a fizz sans sugar) with the addition of grenadine to sweeten it only slightly and give the drink its nice rosy hue. For a longer, cooling drink, pour it into a highball glass and top with a little soda.

---

2 OUNCES TEQUILA

¾ OUNCE LIME JUICE

¾ OUNCE GRENADINE
(PAGE 333)

5 DASHES ANGOSTURA
BITTERS

SODA WATER
(OPTIONAL)

GARNISH
LIME WHEEL

Add all ingredients to a cocktail shaker. Add ice and shake until chilled. Strain into a rocks glass over ice. Garnish with a lime wheel.

MICHELADA

 | **SERVES 1** | ⌞

The origin of the versatile Michelada equation (tomato juice plus citrus plus something spicy plus beer) is hazy. But it is undoubtedly the product of someone who knew his or her way around a hangover. The drink offers the opportunity for tinkering at every ingredient; give it a try with orange juice or with a little soy sauce for an umami infusion—or even a wheat beer to add more body. But the real fun is in testing out different rims, using whatever's in your cabinet. The classic rim is straight up salt and pepper, but Tajín, a chile lime-spiked salt from Mexico, is a pro move, as are smoky barbecue spice blends and even *furikake*, a Japanese combination of seaweed and sesame seeds.

SALT AND PEPPER	5-6 DASHES HOT SAUCE	1 MEXICAN BEER, TO TOP
1 OUNCE LIME JUICE	3 OUNCES TOMATO JUICE	**GARNISH** LIME WEDGE

Rim a pint glass with salt and pepper (see page 29) and fill with ice. Add lime juice, hot sauce, tomato juice, salt, and pepper to the prepared pint glass and top with beer. Garnish with a lime wedge.

MILLIONAIRE COCKTAIL

 **SERVES 1**

The Millionaire is the John Jacob Jingleheimer Schmidt of Prohibition-era drinks. Unsurprisingly, Roaring Twenties bartenders had an affinity for the name, bestowing it upon recipes so distinct from one another that not even the base spirit was consistent. The only through line was that the ingredients were perceived as somewhat flashy at the time. This rendition was inspired by a recipe that appeared in 1938's *The How and When* cocktail book by Hyman Gale and Gerald F. Marco. Here, the proportions have been updated ever so slightly and a little lemon juice added at the recommendation of Jason Kosmas and Dushan Zaric of New York City's Employees Only.

---

2 OUNCES BOURBON, PREFERABLY FOUR ROSES

¾ OUNCE GRAND MARNIER

½ OUNCE GRENADINE (PAGE 333)

½ OUNCE LEMON JUICE

1 EGG WHITE

4 DASHES ABSINTHE

GARNISH FRESHLY GRATED NUTMEG

Add all ingredients to a cocktail shaker. Add ice and shake until chilled. Strain into a chilled coupe or cocktail glass. Garnish with grated nutmeg.

MINT JULEP

 | **SERVES 1** |

The Mint Julep is one of the more powerful cocktails to be associated with contemporary day drinking—an association that, of course, owes much to the Kentucky Derby, where 120,000 juleps are said to be sold every year. Race and hats not withstanding, this all-American drink actually dates back to the eighteenth century. The exact origins and recipe have no doubt inspired countless dissertations, but, in short, it most likely originated in Virginia in the late 1700s, when it was considered an aristocratic drink. (Who else could afford silver tins and a coveted block of ice used simply for crushing?) Bourbon became the preferred spirit only after the Civil War, when the South was impoverished and, thanks to phylloxera, brandy had all but disappeared.

---

1 LARGE MINT SPRIG	2–2½ OUNCES	**GARNISH**
½–¾ OUNCE SIMPLE SYRUP (PAGE 332)	BOURBON, PREFERABLY BONDED	BOUQUET OF MINT

In a julep tin or rocks glass, muddle mint sprig with simple syrup by gently pressing to release oils. Pack the glass with finely crushed ice. Pour in bourbon, and mound more ice into the top of the glass. Spank a mint bouquet by clapping it between your hands to release the oils, and garnish.

MOJITO

 | **SERVES 1** |

A descendant of the Draque—an old Cuban concoction of unrefined rum, cane sugar, and lime juice—the mojito was most likely invented when more delicate white rums entered the market in the mid- to late nineteenth century. The first printed references for the version of the recipe we recognize today date to the 1930s. Theories about the drink's moniker abound: some refer to *mojo*, the Cuban lime seasoning, while another points to a play on *mojado*, the Spanish term for "wet." Thanks to the diaspora of Miami club culture, the mojito enjoyed a surge of popularity in United States in the early 1990s, solidifying its post among classic cocktails. Although the mojito can be a curse when it's made poorly (too sugary or too boozy), it's a sweet-tart lifesaver on a hot day when done well.

2 SPRIGS MINT	1 LIME, QUARTERED	**GARNISH**
2 TEASPOONS SUGAR	2 OUNCES LIGHT RUM	MINT SPRIG AND LIME SLICE
	SODA WATER, TO TOP	

In a Collins glass, add mint sprigs and sugar. Muddle by pressing lightly with a muddler to release oils. Drop in lime quarters and muddle to release juice. Add rum, stir, and add ice. Top with soda water. Garnish with a mint sprig and a lime slice.

MOSCOW MULE

 SERVES 1

Best known for its signature icy copper mug, the Moscow Mule is just about the best thing you can drink on a hot summer day. A member of the buck family of ginger beer–based cocktails, this vodka buck is said to have been created in the early 1940s in the midst of an alcohol-fueled meeting between John G. Martin, an executive at the company that bottled the then-unknown Smirnoff, and Jack Morgan, owner of the Cock 'n' Bull bar in Hollywood and a ginger beer producer. At the same time, the two met Sophie Berezinski, a Russian immigrant who'd just landed in the States, hoping to unload the mugs that her father made in his factory, the Moscow Copper Co. Together, in a move of sheer marketing genius, the three dreamed up an easy-to-make drink using their underperforming products.

---

2 OUNCES VODKA

¾ OUNCE LIME JUICE

4 OUNCES GINGER BEER, PREFERABLY FEVER TREE OR FENTIMANS

GARNISH
LIME WHEEL

Add vodka and lime juice to a copper mule mug or Collins or highball glass. Top with crushed or cracked ice. Top with ginger beer and swizzle with a swizzle stick or barspoon gently to mix. Garnish with a lime wheel.

NEGRONI

 | **SERVES 1** |

Like all good stories, the one about the Negroni involves rakish Italian nobility. Most accounts credit the recipe to one Count Negroni, a swashbuckling proto-boho who reportedly spent time as a rodeo cowboy in the United States. Compounding his wild ways, legend has it that back at a bar in Italy in 1919, he asked for a something like an Americano but boozier. Swap gin for soda water, and presto: the Negroni. Navigating a tightrope between bitter and sweet, this powerful drink—a study in balance—has evolved into one of the cornerstones of the classic cocktail revival.

---

1 OUNCE GIN

1 OUNCE CAMPARI

1 OUNCE SWEET
VERMOUTH

GARNISH
ORANGE PEEL

Add all ingredients to a mixing glass. Add ice and stir until chilled. If on the rocks, strain over ice into a rocks glass. If up, strain into a chilled coupe or cocktail glass. Garnish with an orange peel.

NEGRONI SBAGLIATO

 | **SERVES 1** |

This twist on the Negroni allegedly came to be when a Milanese bartender reached for a bottle of prosecco rather than gin when making the classic drink—the *sbagliato* addendum translates to mean "incorrect" or "mistaken." But, in fact, the buoyantly bitter Italian aperitivo drink is anything but incorrect. If the *sbagliato* is wrong, you don't want to be right.

---

1 OUNCE CAMPARI

1 OUNCE SWEET VERMOUTH

3 OUNCES PROSECCO (OR ANY DRY SPARKLING WINE), TO TOP

GARNISH ORANGE PEEL

In a rocks or lowball glass, add Campari, sweet vermouth, and ice. Top with prosecco (or sparkling wine) and stir gently to combine. Garnish with an orange peel.

NEW YORK SOUR

 | **SERVES 1**

There's nothing remarkably New York about this sour aside from the fact that it aspires to stand out from the rest of the crowd. As if a perfect Whiskey Sour (bourbon or rye, sugar, and lemon juice), shaken and poured over ice with an ample froth, needed any embellishment, the New York version takes it up just one little notch, with a red wine float as the cherry on top. And sure, this colorful flair certainly isn't necessary, but it is *so New York*.

| 2 OUNCES RYE OR BOURBON | 1 OUNCE LEMON JUICE | ¼ OUNCE RED WINE |
| | 1 OUNCE SIMPLE SYRUP (PAGE 332) | |

Add whiskey, lemon juice, and simple syrup to a cocktail shaker. Add ice and shake until chilled. Strain over ice into a rocks glass. Gently pour red wine over the back of a barspoon to create a float atop the cocktail.

OLD PAL

 **SERVES 1**

Certain names come up again and again as the creators of long-beloved drinks—like ghosts sitting at the bar lending guidance and inspiration to today's best bartenders. One such person is Harry MacElhone, an Irish chap who became the proprietor of Harry's Bar in Paris in the 1920s. Just as MacElhone credited his "old pal" William "Sparrow" Robinson, the sports editor for the *New York Herald* in Paris, as the impetus for this drink, numerous bartenders would credit their "old pal" MacElhone for many of theirs. The Old Pal is essentially a Boulevardier (page 59), another MacElhone drink, but drier thanks to dry vermouth in place of sweet vermouth, mixed with rye and Campari.

| 1 OUNCE RYE | 1 OUNCE DRY VERMOUTH | **GARNISH** |
| 1 OUNCE CAMPARI | | LEMON PEEL |

Add all ingredients to a mixing glass. Add ice and stir until chilled. Strain into a chilled coupe or cocktail glass. Garnish with a lemon peel.

OLD-FASHIONED

 | **SERVES 1** |

A simple mix of spirits, sugar, bitters, and water, the old-fashioned made its appearance in 1806 as the first printed recipe for a cocktail ("cock tail"), but it wasn't named until later that century after more ostentatious new-fangled cocktails entered the canon. In fact, during Prohibition, the old-fashioned nearly lost its humble footing when the recipe veered into odd territory, adding fruit and cherries to distract from the available crude spirits. After repeal, the imposter version stuck until the recent cocktail revival brought the original recipe back from the brink of extinction.

| 1 SUGAR CUBE, 1 TEASPOON GRANULATED SUGAR, OR ¼ OUNCE SIMPLE SYRUP (PAGE 332) | 2–3 DASHES ANGOSTURA BITTERS

SPLASH WARM WATER (IF USING SUGAR CUBE OR SUGAR) | 2 OUNCES RYE OR BOURBON

GARNISH ORANGE PEEL |

In a double rocks glass, muddle the sugar cube or sugar with Angostura bitters and a small splash of warm water until dissolved. If using simple syrup, swirl with bitters in a double rocks glass. Add whiskey and ice (preferably an oversize cube) and stir well. Garnish with an orange peel.

PAINKILLER

 | **SERVES 1** |

Plenty of tiki drinks could have a name like Painkiller, with their boozy layers of rum and absurd garnishes. But this one emphasizes the soothing powers of being transported to a tropical island via a single Virgin Islands rum that's mellowed by waves of pineapple juice, orange juice, and coconut cream. The origin of the Painkiller is disputed (though credit is often given to Daphne Henderson of the Soggy Dollar Bar on the British Virgin Island Jost Van Dyke), but what's not argued is who owns the cocktail: Pusser's Rum, which trademarked the name in the 1990s.

1½ OUNCES VIRGIN ISLANDS RUM	½ OUNCE ORANGE JUICE	**GARNISH** FRESHLY GRATED NUTMEG, MINT SPRIG, AND UMBRELLA (OPTIONAL)
1½ OUNCES PINEAPPLE JUICE	¾ OUNCE CREAM OF COCONUT, PREFERABLY COCO LOPEZ	

Add all ingredients to a cocktail shaker and dry shake. Pour into a tiki mug and top with crushed ice. Garnish generously with grated nutmeg, a mint sprig, and an umbrella, if desired.

PALOMA

SERVES 1

A peaceful name for an easygoing Collins, *la paloma* means "the dove" in Spanish. Fizzy and cooling, the Paloma is like the sweet-tart love child of a margarita and a Greyhound. Although not much is known about the drink's provenance, it is undeniable that it's wildly popular—perhaps even more so than the margarita—in its home country, Mexico. Technically a cooler, the simplest version of a Paloma is nothing more than a tall, salt-rimmed glass of tequila, lime juice, and grapefruit-flavored soda like Fresca or Squirt. Here, the soda is swapped for fresh grapefruit, simple syrup, and soda water to allow for more control over the sweetness, plus a couple of dashes of grapefruit bitters to dial up the citrus profile.

2 OUNCES TEQUILA	¾ OUNCE SIMPLE SYRUP (PAGE 332)	SODA WATER, TO TOP
1 OUNCE GRAPEFRUIT JUICE	2 DASHES GRAPEFRUIT BITTERS (OPTIONAL)	**GARNISH** GRAPEFRUIT WHEEL
½ OUNCE LIME JUICE		

Add first four (five if using bitters) ingredients to a cocktail shaker. Add ice and shake until chilled. Strain into a Collins glass over ice. Top with soda water. Garnish with a grapefruit wheel.

PEGU CLUB

 | **SERVES 1** |

As Britain colonized its way across continental Asia in the nineteenth century, residents set up outposts for their empire's wayward explorers in an effort to provide a civilized gathering place after a long day of conquering. Each of these boys' clubs had its own rituals and drinking rites. The Pegu Club, located in Yangon, Myanmar, found itself at the center of British social life in the 1920s. Its members, citizens of a bygone political era, knew the city as Rangoon, Burma, and this drink was their house cocktail. The Pegu Club eventually found its way into 1927's *Barflies and Cocktails* by Harry MacElhone, the owner of Harry's New York Bar in Paris, and was further immortalized by Audrey Saunders's New York City bar, also called Pegu Club.

2 OUNCES LONDON DRY GIN	¾ OUNCE LIME JUICE	1 DASH ORANGE BITTERS
¾ OUNCE DRY CURAÇAO, PREFERABLY PIERRE FERRAND	1 DASH ANGOSTURA BITTERS	**GARNISH** LIME PEEL

Add all ingredients to a cocktail shaker. Add ice and shake until chilled. Strain into a chilled coupe or cocktail glass. Garnish with a lime peel.

NOTE The Pegu Club is an extremely dry cocktail. To add a hint of sweetness, splash in a dash or two of simple syrup (page 332).

PHILADELPHIA FISH HOUSE PUNCH

 | **SERVES 10** |

Philadelphia Fish House Punch was born from a group of rebellious (and most likely overheated) colonial Americans—fishermen, politicians, and Philadelphians of the like—who founded a pre-Revolution social club called the Schuylkill Fishing Company of Pennsylvania. Its constituents actually declared the assemblage a sovereign state and called themselves "citizens." They still do today. Heady and heavy-handed, this punch is made for lazy summer afternoons (or—when heated and mulled—lazy winter weekends), so refrain from following a punch bowl up with any sort of plans, angling or otherwise.

½ CUP SUGAR

2 LEMONS, PEELED AND JUICE RESERVED

2 CUPS BLACK TEA (OR WATER), WARM

2 CUPS JAMAICAN RUM

1 CUP COGNAC

¼ CUP PEACH BRANDY

GARNISH
LEMON WHEELS STUDDED WITH WHOLE CLOVES

In a large bowl, add sugar and lemon peels and rub together to release citrus oils into sugar. Allow to infuse for 30 minutes. Add warm tea (or water) and stir to dissolve sugar. Add rum, Cognac, lemon juice, and peach brandy and stir to mix. Add a block of ice to chill, and add smaller pieces of ice for desired dilution. Garnish with lemon wheels and ladle into individual glasses.

PIMM'S CUP

 | **SERVES 1** |

The summer cup, an adaptable gin-based punch mixed with seasonal fruit and liqueur, has been a part of the English drinking institution since the early 1900s. When Englishman James Pimm invented this version of the crisp cooler (based off his eponymous gin-based liqueur) at his London oyster bar in the mid-nineteenth century, he surely couldn't have imagined that it would become the official cocktail of Wimbledon. Today it is to Wimbledon as the Mint Julep is to the Kentucky Derby. Typically garnished with cucumber spears and either oranges or strawberries, this drink is a blueprint ripe for riffing with additional spirits, seasonal fruit, or large-format batching.

2 OUNCES PIMM'S NO. 1	¼ OUNCE SIMPLE SYRUP (PAGE 332)	**GARNISH** CUCUMBER SPEAR OR SLICE, MINT SPRIG, SEASONAL BERRIES AND CITRUS
½ OUNCE LEMON JUICE	SODA WATER, TO TOP	
	2 DASHES ANGOSTURA BITTERS	

To a Collins glass, add Pimm's, lemon juice, and simple syrup and stir. Add ice, top with soda water and bitters, and stir gently to mix. Garnish lavishly like a flower arrangement with a cucumber slice, fresh mint sprig, berries, and citrus.

PIÑA COLADA

 **SERVES 1**

Based on a Cuban recipe for a nonalcoholic pineapple slushy (a *piña fría*) popular in the early 1900s, this frozen beverage evolved to include coconut cream and rum. The Puerto Rican Hilton claims to have invented the recipe in 1954, but the first-known mention of what we call the piña colada came from the *New York Times* in 1950 and attributed the drink to a bar in Cuba. Immortalized in Warren Zevon's song "Werewolves of London" ("I saw a werewolf drinking a piña colada at Trader Vic's . . .") in 1978 and then again in 1979, with the No. 1 hit single "Escape (The Piña Colada Song)" by Rupert Holmes, the piña colada has long held a place in the public imagination as a fanciful, otherworldly drink.

2 OUNCES RUM, LIGHT OR AGED	1 OUNCE PINEAPPLE JUICE	1 OUNCE COCONUT MILK
½ OUNCE LIME JUICE	1 OUNCE CREAM OF COCONUT	**GARNISH** PINEAPPLE WEDGE AND UMBRELLA

Add all ingredients to a blender with 1 cup of ice. Blend on high until smooth. Pour into a Collins or hurricane glass (or a hollowed-out pineapple). Garnish with a pineapple wedge and an umbrella.

PISCO SOUR

 | **SERVES 1** |

Made with pisco, lemon juice, simple syrup, and egg white, this frothy spur off the sour family tree has roots in both America and Peru. The story goes that American-born Victor Morris moved to Peru in the early twentieth century to work on the railroads but ended up opening a bar instead. He supposedly fashioned an antecedent of what's known as the Pisco Sour, bringing Peru's local liquor to bear on a sour template.

2 OUNCES PISCO	½ OUNCE SIMPLE SYRUP (PAGE 332)	**GARNISH** ANGOSTURA BITTERS
¾ OUNCE LEMON JUICE	½ LARGE OR 1 SMALL EGG WHITE	

Add all ingredients to a cocktail shaker and dry shake. Add ice to the shaker and shake well. Strain into a chilled coupe or cocktail glass. Garnish with a few drops of Angostura bitters.

PLANTER'S PUNCH

 | **SERVES 1** |

Planter's Punch can be traced back to a time when the West Indies were considered exotic and recipes were written in verse. "Two of sour, one and a half of sweet, three of strong and four of weak," directed one description from a 1908 article in the *New York Times*. Ingredient ratios vary from account to account, as does the drink's name—it's been known as Jamaican Rum Punch (*Savoy Cocktail Book*) and Creole Punch (per British novelist Alec Waugh)—but it almost always contains rum, lime, sugar, and water. More modern versions, like the one from tiki stalwart Trader Vic's, include sweeteners such as grenadine, or curaçao.

1½ OUNCES DARK CARIBBEAN RUM	½ OUNCE ORANGE JUICE	**GARNISH** PINEAPPLE SLICE, CITRUS WHEELS, AND/OR MINT SPRIG
½ OUNCE LIME JUICE	¼ OUNCE GRENADINE (PAGE 333)	
1 OUNCE PINEAPPLE JUICE		

Add all ingredients to a cocktail shaker. Add ice and shake until chilled. Strain over ice into a rocks glass. Garnish with a pineapple slice, citrus wheels, and/or mint sprig.

NOTE This cocktail can easily be batched. Just multiply the measurements by the number of servings desired.

QUEEN'S PARK SWIZZLE

 **SERVES 1**

With few ingredients, this drink gets its unique signature from the swizzle technique, which calls for agitating the drink with a swizzle stick (see page 25). Created in Trinidad, the rum-based, bitters-topped drink is named for a famous cricket field in the country's capital, Port of Spain. However, its traditional dark and muggy Demerara rum base hails from neighboring Guyana, which had a more established rum industry than Trinidad when this drink was created in the early twentieth century.

1 LARGE SPRIG MINT

1 OUNCE SIMPLE SYRUP
(PAGE 332)

1 OUNCE
LIME JUICE

2 OUNCES
DEMERARA RUM

4 DASHES
ANGOSTURA BITTERS

GARNISH
MINT SPRIG

In a Collins or hurricane glass, gently muddle mint sprig with simple syrup to release oils. Add lime juice, rum, and crushed ice. Swizzle with a straw or swizzle stick to mix. Add more crushed ice and dash Angostura bitters over the top. Garnish with a mint sprig.

RAMOS GIN FIZZ

 | **SERVES 1** |

Walk into any cocktail bar and order a Ramos Gin Fizz and you'll either be greeted with an eye roll or a delighted bartender eager to shake the hell out of one of the most laborious classics. With a texture somewhere between a Gin Fizz (page 98) and a milk shake, the Ramos was born in New Orleans at Henry Ramos's Imperial Cabinet Saloon in 1888. Ramos wanted the drink to be so foamy and cloudlike that he actually employed a chain of "shaker men" to, one by one, have a go at emulsifying the drink. A perfectly fluffy Ramos Gin Fizz can certainly be made without deploying several dozen shaker men. For the best result, start by giving the drink a good dry shake, then add ice for the second round of agitation.

2 OUNCES GIN	½ OUNCE SIMPLE SYRUP (PAGE 332)	1 EGG WHITE
½ OUNCE LEMON JUICE	3 DASHES ORANGE FLOWER WATER	2 OUNCES SODA WATER
½ OUNCE LIME JUICE	1 OUNCE CREAM	**GARNISH** LIME PEEL

Add all ingredients except soda water to a cocktail shaker. Shake for a full minute without ice. Add ice and shake until well chilled. Strain into a snifter or a Collins glass and top with soda. Garnish with a lime peel.

REMEMBER THE MAINE

 **SERVES 1**

First described by spirits writer Charles H. Baker in his 1939 classic *The Gentleman's Companion, or Around the World with Jigger, Beaker and Flask,* this rye-based drink is part Sazerac, part Manhattan, and part grandiose backstory. The *Maine,* a U.S. naval ship, was sitting off the coast of Havana in 1898 in a bout of saber-rattling with Spain, which controlled Cuba at the time. When the ship mysteriously exploded and sank (some blame a coal fire), warmongering journalists used the phrase "Remember the *Maine,* to Hell with Spain" as a rallying cry that would jump-start the Spanish-American War, which led to Cuba's independence. Baker, however, wrote about the drink in the context of the 1933 Cuban Revolution. Baker happened to be in Havana during "the unpleasantness . . . when each swallow was punctuated with the sound of . . . shells being fired at the Hotel Nacional."

---

1 DASH ABSINTHE	¾ OUNCE SWEET VERMOUTH	**GARNISH**
2 OUNCES RYE		BRANDIED CHERRY, PREFERABLY LUXARDO
	2 TEASPOONS CHERRY HEERING	

To a chilled coupe or cocktail glass, add a dash of absinthe. Roll around to coat and discard excess. Add remaining ingredients to a mixing glass. Add ice and stir well. Strain into the prepared glass. Garnish with a brandied cherry.

ROB ROY

SERVES 1

The Waldorf Astoria hotel's proximity to Broadway theaters provided great cocktail name fodder at the turn of the twentieth century. While some call to mind the theatergoing clientele, others harken back to the plays themselves. The altruistic, kilt-wearing Scotsman protagonist Rob Roy inspired bartenders to swap the rye or bourbon in a Manhattan (page 114) for Scotch whisky. While the eponymous drink references a true renegade, it's actually a touch leaner and meeker than its Manhattan counterpart. Since the Scotch gets fortified with sweet vermouth and bitters, a blended version will more than suffice here.

2 OUNCES SCOTCH, PREFERABLY BLENDED	2 DASHES ANGOSTURA BITTERS	**GARNISH** BRANDIED CHERRY, PREFERABLY LUXARDO, OR LEMON PEEL
1 OUNCE SWEET VERMOUTH		

Add all ingredients to a mixing glass. Add ice and stir until chilled. Strain into a chilled coupe or cocktail glass. Garnish with a brandied cherry or a lemon peel.

NOTE A Rob Roy mixed with Carpano Antica sweet vermouth makes for a nice full-bodied drink, but if you can't find it, Martini & Rossi makes a fine, albeit slightly fruitier, substitute.

SAZERAC

 | **SERVES 1** |

Cocktails born in New Orleans, like the Sazerac and the Vieux Carré (page 194), tell spirited and compelling stories. Born in the mid-1800s at the Sazerac Coffee House, the original Sazerac recipe featured Cognac. But in the late nineteenth century, an outbreak of phylloxera in France's vineyards caused a shortage of grapes, leading to a shortage of Cognac as well. Without access to the original spirit, bartenders substituted the South's ubiquitous rye whiskey as the base. The Sazerac morphed again when absinthe became illegal in 1912, and a local pastis, Herbsaint, was subbed in to approximate the taste of absinthe. The Sazerac's alluring aromatic intensity—anise, peppery rye, and spiced Peychaud's bitters—make this one of the most beloved drinks in the canon of classic cocktails.

---

1 DASH ABSINTHE

1 SUGAR CUBE,
1 TEASPOON
GRANULATED SUGAR,
OR ¼ OUNCE SIMPLE
SYRUP (PAGE 332)

1 SPLASH
SODA WATER

2 OUNCES RYE

2 DASHES
PEYCHAUD'S BITTERS

GARNISH
LEMON PEEL

To a rocks glass, add a dash of absinthe. Swirl to coat and discard excess. In another rocks or mixing glass, muddle sugar cube or sugar with soda water. Once dissolved, add rye, bitters, and ice and stir well. Strain into the prepared rocks glass. Garnish with a lemon peel.

SCORPION BOWL

 | **SERVES 4** |

The Scorpion, like many tiki cocktails, has gone through countless iterations, from a gin-and-wine-laced punch to this contemporary version of Trader Vic's 1946 recipe. It's difficult to know where the original recipe ends and the contemporary one begins, especially when so much rum is involved. But it is thought that, while in Hawaii, Vic first tried the punch from which the Scorpion was modeled, which mostly likely contained *okolehao*, an indigenous spirit distilled from the Polynesian ti plant. Orgeat, a syrup made from almonds, is a constant ingredient in most interpretations and is key to the balance of dark rum and fruit.

---

10 OUNCES AÑEJO RUM

2 OUNCES COGNAC

3 OUNCES ORGEAT

4 OUNCES
LEMON JUICE

3 OUNCES
ORANGE JUICE

GARNISH
FRESHLY GRATED
CINNAMON, CINNAMON
STICKS, GRAPEFRUIT
PEEL, ORCHIDS, AND/OR
FLAMING LIME SHELL

Add all ingredients to a blender with 1 cup crushed ice. Blend quickly and pour into a Scorpion bowl, or portion out into individual tiki mugs. Add several large ice cubes to bowl or mugs. To garnish, add freshly grated cinnamon, cinnamon sticks, a grapefruit peel, orchids, or flaming lime peel. Serve with straws.

SHERRY COBBLER

 | **SERVES 1** |

By most accounts, the Sherry Cobbler is an American-born cocktail, thought to have originated sometime in the 1820s or early 1830s. But like most nineteenth-century drinks, its origins are foggy. Its great launching pad to international renown came courtesy of Charles Dickens and his *Life and Adventures of Martin Chuzzlewit* (1843–44). In a scene now famous among cocktail dorks, Chuzzlewit, reacting to his first Sherry Cobbler, sums up the nineteenth-century sentiment around the drink: "Martin took the glass with an astonished look; applied his lips to the reed; and cast up his eyes once in ecstasy. He paused no more until the goblet was drained to the last drop. 'This wonderful invention, sir,' said Mark, tenderly patting the empty glass, 'is called a cobbler.'"

2–3 ORANGE SLICES	3½ OUNCES	**GARNISH**
1 TABLESPOON SUGAR	SHERRY, PREFERABLY AMONTILLADO	SEASONAL BERRIES AND MINT

Add orange slices and sugar to a mixing tin and muddle. Add sherry and ice and shake. Strain into a Collins glass filled with crushed ice. Garnish with seasonal berries, mint, and a straw.

NOTE Don't feel limited by the recommendation of using orange slices here. The Sherry Cobbler is made better when it's loaded up with seasonal fruit. For other variations, switch up the type of sherry and adjust the sugar to your taste.

SHERRY FLIP

 **SERVES 1**

The flip has made a comeback of late, with bartenders testing out stout beer (to make an especially frothy version), rum (more complex flavor), or brandy (for a big kick). But it's the deep, nutty character of dry oloroso sherry—and its higher level of glycerol, which gives it great viscosity—combined with the creaminess of an entire egg that evokes what Jerry Thomas, in his 1887 version of *How to Mix Drinks*, aptly described as a "very delicious drink" that "gives strength to delicate people." Sure does. A cold weather fortifier, the Sherry Flip can serve as a less polarizing—and less boozy—stand-in for eggnog at holiday time.

2 OUNCES OLOROSO SHERRY	½ OUNCE SIMPLE SYRUP OR DEMERARA SYRUP (PAGE 232)	**GARNISH** FRESHLY GRATED NUTMEG
	1 EGG	

Add all ingredients to a shaker and dry shake vigorously for 30 seconds. Add ice and shake for another 30 seconds. Strain into a coupe or small wineglass. Garnish with freshly grated nutmeg.

SIDECAR

 **SERVES 1**

The sidecar often plays second fiddle to many other classic drinks, probably because the proper ratio of Cognac to Cointreau to lemon is nearly impossible to get right—one flavor almost always sticks out more than the others. And yet, when that sweet spot is found, there's nothing better than a sidecar. Although its birthplace is unknown (London? Paris?), the inspiration for the cocktail almost certainly comes from the Brandy Crusta, a Cognac-based variation on the old-fashioned created in New Orleans in the mid-nineteenth century. It can also be considered a Cognac sour in which simple syrup is replaced with Cointreau. Today, sidecars tend to be served with a quirky sugared rim that's most likely a borrowed trick from the Crusta, which only started showing up in written sidecar recipes in the 1930s (and then stuck).

---

2 OUNCES COGNAC (VS OR VSOP)	¾ OUNCE LEMON JUICE	**GARNISH** SUGAR RIM (OPTIONAL) AND AN ORANGE PEEL
¾ OUNCE COINTREAU		

Rim a coupe or cocktail glass with sugar, if desired (see page 29). Add all ingredients to a cocktail shaker. Add ice and shake until chilled. Strain into the prepared glass. Garnish with an orange peel.

SINGAPORE SLING

 | **SERVES 1** |

As one of the oldest drink formulas in existence, the basic sling was originally composed simply of spirits, water, and a sweetener. More a tiki-fied punch than a sling, the Singapore Sling was created at the Raffles Hotel in 1915 in balmy Singapore. At that time, it was most likely nothing more than gin, citrus, soda water, and cherry brandy. Over the years, though, it went through a number of hyperbolically sweet phases, some including prebottled mixers and canned juices. Today, the Singapore Sling has been dialed back to its drier incarnation using fresh lime juice and cherry brandy.

1½ OUNCES GIN, LONDON DRY

¼ OUNCE CHERRY HEERING

¼ OUNCE COINTREAU

¼ OUNCE BÉNÉDICTINE

¼ OUNCE GRENADINE (PAGE 333)

1 OUNCE LIME JUICE

¾ OUNCE PINEAPPLE JUICE

1 DASH ANGOSTURA BITTERS

2 OUNCES SODA WATER

GARNISH
BRANDIED CHERRY, PINEAPPLE WEDGE, AND A SPRIG OF MINT

Add all ingredients, except soda water, to a cocktail shaker. Add ice and shake until chilled. Strain over ice into a Collins glass. Top with soda. Garnish with a brandied cherry, a pineapple wedge, and a mint sprig.

SLOE GIN FIZZ

 SERVES 1

Until recently, sloe gin was best known as the base for such absurdly named collegiate classics as the Alabama Slammer and the Sloe Comfortable Screw. However, the purple stuff that spilled across American campuses in the 1980s and 1990s was merely a fruitier imposter of the proper British-style sloe gin. Luckily, the classic SGF is enjoying a renaissance in the United States with the return of true sloe gin—a mixture of English blackthorn sloe berries (a more petite relative of the plum) macerated in gin. This version of the Sloe Gin Fizz is slightly unorthodox in its use of a blend of regular gin and sloe gin, plus the (optional) addition of an egg white for a bit of fluffy oomph.

1 OUNCE SODA WATER

¾ OUNCE SLOE GIN, PREFERABLY PLYMOUTH

¾ OUNCE GIN

¾ OUNCE LEMON JUICE

½ OUNCE SIMPLE SYRUP (PAGE 332)

1 EGG WHITE (OPTIONAL)

Add soda water to a coupe or fizz glass. Add sloe gin, gin, lemon juice, simple syrup, and egg white, if desired, to a cocktail shaker and dry shake. Add ice and shake until well chilled. Strain into the prepared glass on top of the soda and observe the fluffy foam.

SOUTHSIDE

 | **SERVES 1**

Depending on how you look at the glass, the Southside lands somewhere between a Gin Mojito sans soda water and a Gimlet (page 92) with mint. Though New York's 21 Club lays claim to the recipe as part of its Prohibition-era menu, some cocktail historians place its conception some forty years earlier at the Southside Sportsmen's Club, a private establishment on Long Island where tony Manhattanites went to hunt, fish, and drink Mint Juleps—the drink that probably inspired this iteration. The clubby association stuck, and the drink became standard issue for the pearls and nine-iron set, but its light, breezy personality makes it a good conversationalist in any setting.

6–8 MINT LEAVES	2 OUNCES GIN	1 DASH ORANGE BITTERS
¾ OUNCE SIMPLE SYRUP (PAGE 332)	¾ OUNCE LIME JUICE	**GARNISH** MINT SPRIG

In a cocktail shaker, gently muddle mint leaves with simple syrup. Add all other ingredients, and ice, and shake until chilled. Double strain into a chilled coupe or cocktail glass. Spank a mint sprig by clapping it between your hands to release the oils and garnish.

NOTE London-style dry gin plays nice in Southsides, especially this version. If you've got it, use it.

STONE FENCE

 | **SERVES 1** |

Before raiding Fort Ticonderoga at the beginning of the Revolutionary War in 1775, Ethan Allen and the Green Mountain Boys went drinking at the Remington Tavern in Castleton, where they knocked back a mixture of rum and hard cider. Finding only a few dozing guards at the fort, Allen stormed the officers' quarters and demanded they surrender "in the name of the Great Jehovah and the Continental Congress." The English didn't offer Allen much resistance, and Fort Ticonderoga was successfully seized, perhaps thanks to the blood-warming Stone Fence. In Allen's day, rum and hard cider surely were the backbone of this drink, but as time went on, whiskey production outpaced that of rum. This version can be tweaked to include rum, brandy, or whiskey. The folks at the whiskey-centric Southern Efficiency in Washington, D.C., astutely suggest the addition of mint and Angostura bitters.

---

2 OUNCES DARK RUM, BRANDY, BOURBON, OR RYE

1 DASH ANGOSTURA BITTERS

5 OUNCES FRESH-PRESSED APPLE CIDER

GARNISH
MINT SPRIG OR FRESHLY GRATED NUTMEG

Add all ingredients to a rocks glass over ice. Garnish with a mint sprig or freshly grated nutmeg.

TI' PUNCH

 | **SERVES 1** |

The Ti' Punch is Martinique's national cocktail, the island's answer to America's Old-Fashioned. Traditionally, the drink (pronounced "tee paunch" in the Caribbean—*ti'* being the Creole variant of the French *petit*) includes a heavy dose of Martinique's rhum agricole, a grassy, fragrant rum made from ultrafresh sugarcane juice, rounded out with a touch of lime juice and a splash of cane syrup (made from the same juice the rum is made with). Simple syrup will do perfectly well in a pinch.

---

1 SPLASH CANE SYRUP
OR SIMPLE SYRUP
(PAGE 332)

1 WEDGE LIME

2 OUNCES RHUM
AGRICOLE, LIGHT
OR DARK

GARNISH
LIME PEEL COIN

In a rocks glass, add cane syrup and a squeeze of lime. Add rhum agricole and a few ice cubes. Stir gently and garnish with a lime coin.

TOM COLLINS

 **SERVES 1**

The American side of the story goes that the Tom Collins evolved from the "The Great Tom Collins Hoax" of 1874, in which pranksters would tell a friend they had run into one "Tom Collins" at a bar around the corner and that he'd said some slanderous things about said friend. Said friend would then leave to hunt down "Tom Collins" at the bar around the corner, sparking a goose chase of perhaps not-so-epic proportions. But there's also the British side, which (more likely) suggests that the Tom Collins was the creation of London bartender John Collins, who dreamed up an eponymous gin punch in the latter half of the nineteenth century, and, when made with Old Tom Gin, presumably became the Tom Collins. The first published recipe appears in Jerry Thomas's 1876 *The Bartender's Guide*. By either route (or perhaps a combination of the two), the Tom Collins is a spritzy drink made of lemon, sugar, soda water, and gin—which combine to form, what is, essentially, the original hard lemonade.

1½ OUNCES GIN	¾ OUNCE SIMPLE SYRUP (PAGE 332)	**GARNISH**
¾ OUNCE LEMON JUICE	SODA WATER, TO TOP	BRANDIED CHERRY (PREFERABLY LUXARDO) AND AN ORANGE WHEEL

Add gin, lemon juice, and simple syrup to a cocktail shaker. Add ice and shake until chilled. Strain over ice into a Collins glass. Top with soda water. Garnish with a brandied cherry and an orange wheel.

TUXEDO

 **SERVES 1**

There are a dozen or so sherry and gin drinks that start to pop up during the twilight years of the nineteenth century and repeat themselves with very slight variations throughout the beginning of the twentieth. Of them all, the Tuxedo, a Martini (page 121) variation that trades sherry for dry vermouth, is the best and most well known. The drink's name refers to the Tuxedo Park, a sort of early experiment in country club living established in 1886 in Orange County, New York, about 40 miles north of New York City. Tuxedo Park was the birthplace of not only the first complete sewage system in America but also the tail-less suit, which was called, yes, the tuxedo. The members of this bougie utopia were known as Tuxedoites and, before shuffling out of the city after work, they no doubt stopped off at the city's top bars, most notable among them the Waldorf Astoria bar, where this drink was born.

---

2 OUNCES GIN, PREFERABLY PLYMOUTH OR BEEFEATER 24

1 OUNCE FINO SHERRY, PREFERABLY LA INA

2 DASHES REGANS' ORANGE BITTERS

GARNISH
ORANGE PEEL

Add all ingredients to a mixing glass. Add ice and stir well. Strain into a chilled coupe or cocktail glass. Garnish with an orange peel.

VESPER

 | **SERVES 1** |

James Bond may not have invented the martini, but he was the first bar-goer on record to order the drink in Ian Fleming's first Bond novel, 1953's *Casino Royale*. In it, the protagonist calls for a strong formula of vodka, gin, and Kina Lillet, "shaken, not stirred," and names the drink for Vesper Lynd, his first and potentially only true love in the series. While Bond fans know his infallibility, cocktail historians have called into question his specification of Kina Lillet—a quinine-infused white wine aperitif whose distillery also produced vermouth—suspecting that he may have intended to use vermouth all along. In the 1980s, the recipe for Lillet became much lighter and sweeter and included less quinine. In order to not squash the delicacy of the Lillet, we've upped its proportion in the drink a bit. That said, Cocchi Americano, a bittersweet Italian aperitivo, is probably the closest substitute for the Kina Lillet of days gone by. Blasphemous though it may be, while Bond said "shake," we most definitely say "stir" to retain the silky texture of the all-spirits drink.

3 OUNCES GIN	½ – ¾ OUNCE LILLET BLANC OR ½ OUNCE COCCHI AMERICANO	**GARNISH** LEMON PEEL
1 OUNCE VODKA		

Add all ingredients to a mixing glass. Add ice and stir well. Strain into a chilled coupe or cocktail glass. Garnish with a lemon peel.

VIEUX CARRÉ

 | **SERVES 1** |

New Orleans does strong and stirred better than most American cities do. From the Hurricane to the Sazerac, Pat O'Brien's to the Napoleon House, much of the Big Easy's cocktail history insists upon specific coordinates of conception. Stanley Clisby Arthur, author of *Famous New Orleans Drinks and How to Mix 'Em*, attributed this drink's original recipe to the Hotel Monteleone, located in the Vieux Carré (French Quarter). Today, the cocktail remains a New Orleans classic and can be enjoyed at its original post at the Monteleone's Carousel Bar, which turns around slowly as life in the peculiar precinct passes by on Royal Street.

---

1 OUNCE RYE	¼ OUNCE BÉNÉDICTINE	2 DASHES ANGOSTURA BITTERS
1 OUNCE COGNAC		
1 OUNCE SWEET VERMOUTH	2 DASHES PEYCHAUD'S BITTERS	**GARNISH** ORANGE OR LEMON PEEL

Add all ingredients to a mixing glass. Add ice and stir until chilled. Strain over ice into a rocks glass. Garnish with an orange or a lemon peel.

WHISKEY SMASH

 | **SERVES 1** |

The layman's Mint Julep, the Whiskey Smash comes with all the flavor of its more famous relative but without the associated frippery (such as tin cups, Derby hats, and more). Jerry Thomas, a nineteenth-century New York bartender, "father of American mixology," and author of the seminal *The Bartender's Guide*, called it "the Julep on a small plan." A few slices of muddled lemon and a fistful of mint help lift and brighten the flavors, making this potent number dangerously easy to toss back.

1 SPRIG MINT	2 LEMON WHEELS	**GARNISH** MINT SPRIG AND LEMON WHEEL
2 DASHES SIMPLE SYRUP (PAGE 332)	1½ OUNCES BOURBON OR RYE	

In a Collins or rocks glass, gently muddle mint with simple syrup to release oils. Add lemon wheels and muddle to release juice. Add crushed ice or small ice cubes and pour bourbon over. Swizzle gently with a barspoon or swizzle stick to mix. Garnish with a mint spring and a lemon wheel.

WHISKEY SOUR

 | **SERVES 1**

The template for this iconic sour—whiskey, lemon juice, and sugar, shaken over ice—has laid the foundation for many cocktails due to its structural, unadorned simplicity. Most bartenders will kick the drink up with the dramatic flourish of an herbal or fruit liqueur, which gives nice complexity, but the Whiskey Sour isn't begging for all that adornment. Merely adding an egg white (creating what's known as a Boston Sour) can take the concoction to a new fluffed-up, ethereal place. For a more vibrant route, top with a red wine float to transform it into the New York Sour (page 138), a variation that popped up in the late 1800s.

---

2 OUNCES BOURBON

¾ OUNCE
LEMON JUICE

¾ OUNCE SIMPLE
SYRUP (PAGE 332)

½ OUNCE OR 1 SMALL
EGG WHITE (OPTIONAL)

Add all ingredients to a cocktail shaker, and dry shake. Add ice to the shaker and shake well. Strain into a chilled coupe or cocktail glass or over ice into a rocks glass.

ZOMBIE

 SERVES 1

Largely considered the founder of tiki cocktail culture, Donn Beach, better known as Don the Beachcomber, opened his eponymous bar in Hollywood in 1934 and created a canon of drinks built upon the base of fresh juices, exotic fruits, complex syrups, and lots and lots of rum. The Zombie is a prime example of his typical concoction: strong and rather mysterious (it contains two different proprietary mixes). Bar lore says the original was so potent that Beach limited his customers to no more than two Zombies in one sitting. This recipe is Beach's original from 1934, as translated by Jeff "Beachbum Berry" in his book *Sippin' Safari*.

1½ OUNCES
JAMAICAN RUM

1½ OUNCES PUERTO
RICAN RUM

1 OUNCE
151-PROOF RUM

½ OUNCE DON'S MIX
(SEE NOTE)

½ OUNCE VELVET
FALERNUM

¾ OUNCE LIME JUICE

¼ OUNCE GRENADINE
(PAGE 333)

2 DASHES ABSINTHE

1 DASH ANGOSTURA
BITTERS

GARNISH
MINT SPRIG

Add all ingredients to a cocktail shaker. Shake with a few ice cubes. Strain into a tiki mug over crushed ice. Garnish with a mint sprig.

NOTE To make Don's Mix, combine 2 parts grapefruit juice with 1 part cinnamon syrup (page 333). Store in an airtight container in the refrigerator until ready to use.

modern
RECIPES

AMERICAN TRILOGY

 | **SERVES 1** |

RICHARD BOCCATO AND MICHAEL MCILROY, NEW YORK, NY

The Old-Fashioned (page 142) is indisputably the emblem of the Prohibition-era cocktail renaissance of the past fifteen years. In that time, it has seen loads of riffs and iterations—and an entire book devoted to it. Most often, bartenders tinker with the drink by swapping out the base spirit (whiskey) for something else, be it mezcal, aged rum, or another spirit, and leave the rest alone. However, when Richard Boccato and Michael McIlroy worked together at Little Branch in New York City, they collaborated to tweak every element, taking the drink to a deeper, darker place. They split the rye with applejack, used a brown sugar cube for richness, gave it some lift with orange bitters, and named it after an Elvis song. Can't get much more American than that.

| 1 BROWN SUGAR CUBE | 1 OUNCE RYE | **GARNISH** |
| 2 DASHES ORANGE BITTERS | 1 OUNCE APPLEJACK, BONDED | LONG, CURLY ORANGE PEEL |

Add sugar cube to a rocks glass and saturate with orange bitters. Gently muddle to make a granulated paste. Add rye, applejack, and ice (preferably an oversize cube). Garnish with a long, curly orange peel.

AMERICANO PERFECTO

 **SERVES 1**

DAMON BOELTE, GRAND ARMY BAR, BROOKLYN, NY

The Italians may have invented the Americano (page 38)—Campari, sweet vermouth, and soda water—but it took pure American ingenuity to add beer to it. Brooklyn's Damon Boelte made this shandy version by replacing the classic aperitif's usual soda water with Einbecker, an ultracrisp German pilsner. The original recipe calls for equal parts Campari and sweet vermouth, and while Boelte holds true to that, he actually uses two different vermouths. "Carpano can be too much, and Dolin can be too little, but I love the botanicals in both," he says. "Together, they make a lovely, balanced sweet vermouth."

1½ OUNCES CAMPARI

¾ OUNCE DOLIN ROUGE SWEET VERMOUTH

¾ OUNCE CARPANO ANTICA SWEET VERMOUTH

4 OUNCES PILSNER

GARNISH
ORANGE WHEEL

Add ice to a Collins glass. Add Campari and both vermouths. Top with pilsner and garnish with an orange wheel.

ANGOSTURA COLADA

 | **SERVES 1** |

ZAC OVERMAN, L'OURSIN, SEATTLE, WA

A new wave of coladas has begun to crop up that all swap the usual rum base for something with more complex spice or herbal flavors. Here, Zac Overman replaces most of the rum with Angostura bitters—and not just a few dashes but a whole 1½ ounces of them. "Angostura bitters have everything you're looking for in a good tiki cocktail—layers and layers of flavor, warm exotic spices, high proof. I sort of look at it like a supercharged spiced rum," Overman says. A bit of lime and overproof rum smooth out and balance the lip-curling bitters, while pineapple and cream of coconut maintain the drink's tropical spirit.

1½ OUNCES ANGOSTURA BITTERS	2 OUNCES PINEAPPLE JUICE	1 OUNCE LIME JUICE
½ OUNCE OVERPROOF RUM, PREFERABLY SMITH & CROSS	1½ OUNCES CREAM OF COCONUT	**GARNISH** ORANGE SLICE, PINEAPPLE LEAVES, FRESHLY GRATED NUTMEG, AND AN UMBRELLA

Add all ingredients to a cocktail shaker. Add ice and shake until chilled. Pour into a snifter and fill with crushed ice. Stir gently and garnish with an orange slice, pineapple leaves, freshly grated nutmeg, and an umbrella.

ARCHANGEL

SERVES 1

RICHARD BOCCATO AND MICHAEL MCILROY, NEW YORK, NY

Leave it to the gin-obsessed British to take a glug of Plymouth, drop in a few dashes of Angostura bitters, and call it a cocktail. The bartender who came up with it in the mid-1800s even went so far as to give the drink a completely obvious name: Pink Gin. Despite its pretty color, it wouldn't be all that palatable for most modern drinkers. Enter Michael McIlroy, and a version that absolutely is. Here, McIlroy uses Aperol to bring the bitterness— and the color. It may be pink, but it's got serious heat.

2 SLICES CUCUMBER	2¼ OUNCES GIN	**GARNISH**
	¾ OUNCE APEROL	LEMON PEEL

In a mixing glass, bruise cucumber slices with a muddler. Add gin, Aperol, and ice and stir until chilled. Strain into a chilled flute or cocktail glass. Garnish with a lemon peel.

BARBER OF SEVILLE

 | **SERVES 1** |

WILL ELLIOTT, MAISON PREMIERE AND SAUVAGE, BROOKLYN, NY

Named for the nineteenth-century Rossini opera, the Barber of Seville is what Will Elliott calls an inverted julep or a sherry swizzle with a rye accent. In a true case of necessity serving as the mother of invention, Elliott created this by playing around with the only bottles he had at home one night. When he mixed rye, sherry, Cappelletti, and some orgeat, he was surprised by the fact that the drink tasted like something you'd get in a bakery. "There was a hint of salinity from the manzanilla, a cereal taste from the rye, and a hint of orange flower water, as used in Italian baked goods, from the orgeat," he says.

---

1 OUNCE MANZANILLA SHERRY, PREFERABLY HIDALGO

½ OUNCE RYE, PREFERABLY OLD OVERHOLT

¾ OUNCE APERITIVO CAPPELLETTI

½ OUNCE LEMON JUICE

¼ OUNCE ORGEAT

½ EYEDROPPER VIAL ORANGE FLOWER WATER

3 DASHES ORANGE BITTERS

GARNISH CRUSHED MARCONA ALMONDS AND FINE ORANGE ZEST

Add all ingredients to a cocktail shaker. Add ice and shake until chilled. Strain into a rocks glass or julep tin and top with crushed ice. Garnish with crushed Marcona almonds and fine orange zest.

BENTON'S OLD-FASHIONED

 | **SERVES 1** |

DON LEE, NEW YORK, NY

This love child of breakfast and the classic old-fashioned came into being when bartender Don Lee lost his mind for the epic smoky bacon from Benton's in Madisonville, Tennessee. Using a method called fat-washing (a means of infusing spirits with cooking fat), bourbon became Lee's vehicle to get that flavor into a drink. Riffing on the flavors of an American breakfast, he created an old-fashioned with rich maple syrup and an orange garnish designed to emulate a sip of OJ.

2 OUNCES BENTON'S BACON FAT-INFUSED BOURBON (SEE NOTE)	¼ OUNCE GRADE B MAPLE SYRUP 2 DASHES ANGOSTURA BITTERS	**GARNISH** ORANGE PEEL

Add all ingredients to a mixing glass. Add ice and stir until chilled. Strain into a rocks glass over ice (preferably a large cube). Garnish with an orange peel.

NOTE To fat-wash bourbon with bacon, over low heat, warm 1½ ounces bacon fat (preferably Benton's, or another thick-cut bacon) in a small saucepan. Stir until it melts, about 5 minutes. Combine the molten fat with 750 ml bourbon in a large nonreactive container and stir. Infuse for 4 hours, then place the container in the freezer for 2 hours. Remove the solid fat, fine-strain the bourbon through a terry cloth or cheesecloth, bottle, and refrigerate.

BITTER INTENTIONS

 **SERVES 1**

BOBBY HEUGEL, ANVIL, HOUSTON, TX

The Bitter Intentions is bartender Bobby Heugel's proof that beautiful things can happen when you embrace bitter in an atypical way. In this case, he uses Campari as if it were gin. In doing so, this Collins-meets-Americano points to the deceptiveness of a classic aperitivo. While Campari is widely used in drinks for its bitter properties, when combined with citrus its own citrusy side is revealed. Heugel calls on the liqueur's sweet notes by matching it with the vanilla flavors of Carpano Antica vermouth.

1½ OUNCES
SODA WATER

2 OUNCES CAMPARI

¾ OUNCE
LEMON JUICE

¾ OUNCE SIMPLE
SYRUP (PAGE 332)

1 OUNCE VERMOUTH,
PREFERABLY
CARPANO ANTICA

GARNISH
ORANGE SLICE

Pour soda water into a Collins glass without ice. Add Campari, lemon juice, and simple syrup to a cocktail shaker. Add ice and shake until cold. Strain into the prepared glass and fill with cracked ice. Top with vermouth and garnish with an orange slice.

BITTER MAI TAI

 | **SERVES 1** |

JEREMY OERTEL, DONNA, BROOKLYN, NY

While bartending at the Brooklyn bar Dram, Jeremy Oertel threw a party with noted tiki bartender Brian Miller. For the occasion, he wanted to replicate a Mai Tai variation he'd come across that used spicy high-proof Angostura bitters in place of rum. But because bitters are a pricy ingredient to use in liberal quantities, he substituted Campari for the bitter component. "It's bitter, but it also has a lot of great fruity flavors, especially grapefruit, so it plays well with the flavors you typically find in tiki cocktails," Oertel says. Here, he uses Smith & Cross Jamaican rum for a heavy funkiness.

1½ OUNCES CAMPARI

¾ OUNCE JAMAICAN RUM, PREFERABLY SMITH & CROSS

½ OUNCE ORANGE CURAÇAO

1 OUNCE LIME JUICE

¾ OUNCE ORGEAT

GARNISH
MINT SPRIG

Add all ingredients to a cocktail shaker. Add a small amount of ice and shake. Strain over crushed ice into a rocks glass. Top with more crushed ice and garnish with a mint sprig.

BITTER TOM

 **SERVES 1**

BRAD FARRAN, BULL DURHAM BEER CO., DURHAM, NC

The Bitter Tom came to be when Brad Farran, then behind the bar at Brooklyn's Clover Club, was attempting to make some sort of Collins to round out his menu. "The original Collins is a marvel of simple ingredients that yield a flavor greater than the sum of its parts," says Farran. "There's a special challenge in creating a new Collins because it's a long drink. There's so much stretching with soda; how do you impart the pop of flavor that makes the drink three-dimensional?" It was a glug of sweet, tangy pomegranate molasses that proved to be the linchpin of the drink, giving it texture, acidity, and flavor in the face of soda water.

2 OUNCES GIN, PREFERABLY TANQUERAY	½ OUNCE SIMPLE SYRUP (PAGE 332)	1 TEASPOON POMEGRANATE MOLASSES
½ OUNCE CAMPARI	1 TEASPOON BÉNÉDICTINE	1 OUNCE SODA WATER
¾ OUNCE LEMON JUICE		**GARNISH** GRAPEFRUIT PEEL

Add all ingredients except soda water to a cocktail shaker. Add ice and roll back and forth from shaker tin to shaker tin. Strain over ice into a Collins glass. Top with soda water and garnish with a grapefruit peel.

BOO RADLEY

 **SERVES 1**

CHRIS HANNAH, FRENCH 75, NEW ORLEANS, LA

Named after the mysterious neighbor in Harper Lee's great
Southern novel, *To Kill a Mockingbird*, the Boo Radley is a play
on another more obscure Southern classic, the Creole cocktail.
Though not Southern in origin—it first appeared as a Manhattan
riff in Hugo Ensslin's *Recipes for Mixed Drinks* in 1916—the Creole's
namesake certainly relates to Louisiana's heritage, which is why
Chris Hannah of French 75 in New Orleans used it as a blueprint.
"Boo was supposed to be the dramatic example of what evil can
do to the innocent and good," says Hannah. "It balanced. I like to
think the bitter in this drink, which is the Cynar, balances with the
sweet and innocent, obviously the Cherry Heering," he says.

2 OUNCES BOURBON	½ OUNCE CHERRY HEERING	**GARNISH**
¾ OUNCE CYNAR		LEMON AND ORANGE PEELS (OPTIONAL)

Add all ingredients to a mixing glass. Add ice and stir until chilled.
Strain into a chilled coupe or cocktail glass. Express (twist to release
the flavorful oils) a lemon peel and an orange peel over cocktail.
Garnish with citrus peels, if desired.

BRAMBLE

 | **SERVES 1** |

Dick Bradsell, one of the founding fathers of London's modern cocktail scene, created this recipe in 1984 when he was working at Fred's Club in Soho. It's essentially a Gin Sour dressed up like a cobbler, but Bradsell considers it a sentimental play on a Singapore Sling (page 178) using entirely British products, with the blackberries and crème de mûre (blackberry liqueur) lending a flavor "reminiscent of his childhood on the Isle of Wight."

---

2 OUNCES GIN

¾ OUNCE
LEMON JUICE

¼ OUNCE SIMPLE
SYRUP (PAGE 332)

½ OUNCE
CRÈME DE MÛRE

GARNISH
BLACKBERRIES AND
LEMON SLICE

Add gin, lemon juice, and simple syrup to a cocktail shaker. Add ice and shake until chilled. Strain over crushed ice into a rocks glass. Drizzle crème de mûre over top, and garnish with blackberries and lemon slice.

NOTE When blackberries are fresh at the farmers' market, omit the crème de mûre and instead muddle 5 or 6 berries with ¾ ounce simple syrup in the shaker before adding the gin and lemon juice. This drink is equally great made with fresh raspberries.

BRANCOLADA

 **SERVES 1**

JEREMY OERTEL, DONNA, BROOKLYN, NY

The Brancolada was born from the idea of a slushy, summery Fernet Branca Menta–infused dessert drink, inspired by pre-shift bar shenanigans. "When I worked at Dram, we had a Branca Menta chilling machine," says Brooklyn bartender Jeremy Oertel. "One of our cocktail waitresses used to bring in ice cream sandwiches, and we'd drizzle it over the top." A play on the traditional Piña Colada (page 154), the Italy-meets-the-tropics Brancolada is a creamy melding of orange and pineapple juices, golden rum, coconut milk, and cool Branca Menta.

---

1 OUNCE FERNET BRANCA MENTA

1 OUNCE JAMAICAN RUM, PREFERABLY APPLETON ESTATE VX RESERVE

1½ OUNCES PINEAPPLE JUICE

¼ OUNCE ORANGE JUICE

1 OUNCE COCONUT CREAM (3 PARTS COCO LOPEZ CREAM OF COCONUT TO 1 PART COCONUT MILK)

GARNISH
MINT SPRIG AND ORANGE SLICE

Add all ingredients to a blender and add 1½ to 2 cups ice. Blend until smooth and pour into a hurricane glass. Garnish with a mint spring and an orange slice.

NOTE Start with less ice; add more as you blend until you've achieved your preferred texture.

CAMPARI RADLER

 | **SERVES 1**

ALEX DAY, PROPRIETORS LLC

On its own, a radler—a combination of fruit soda and beer—is just about the most perfect thing you can drink on a hot summer day. Alex Day's Campari Radler doubles down on the citrus, thanks to a combination of an Austrian grapefruit-flavored radler and lemon juice, and is spiked with bittersweet Campari, yielding a kind of sudsy Americano.

| 1 OUNCE CAMPARI | ¼ OUNCE LEMON JUICE | 1 CAN STIEGL GRAPEFRUIT RADLER OR ANY OTHER RADLER, TO TOP |

Add Campari and lemon juice to a chilled pint glass, and top with beer.

CHARTREUSE SWIZZLE

 **SERVES 1**

MARCO DIONYSOS, SMUGGLER'S COVE, SAN FRANCISCO, CA

A swizzle for the twenty-first century, this tall, frosty cocktail rejiggers the traditional Caribbean Rum Swizzle by basing the drink in green Chartreuse, a lime-colored herbal French liqueur. And though the cocktail is a seemingly odd combination of ingredients, Chartreuse's aromatics pair seamlessly with the spiced falernum and sweet, tropical pineapple. Tangy lime and a pile of crushed ice balance the formula and turn it a springy pastel green. Marco Dionysos created the drink for a Green Chartreuse competition in 2003 and it has found a huge fan base with bartenders around the world. By his count, his Chartreuse Swizzle has made an appearance on more than 130 menus globally.

1¼ OUNCES GREEN CHARTREUSE	1 OUNCE PINEAPPLE JUICE	**GARNISH** LIME WHEELS, PINEAPPLE SPEAR, AND PINEAPPLE LEAF
½ OUNCE VELVET FALERNUM	¾ OUNCE LIME JUICE	

Add all ingredients to a cocktail shaker. Add ice and shake until chilled. Strain into a Collins or pint glass over ice. Garnish with lime wheels, a pineapple spear, and a pineapple leaf.

COSMOPOLITAN

 | **SERVES 1**

TOBY CECCHINI, LONG ISLAND BAR, BROOKLYN, NY

Before the "cosmo" became the must-have liquid accessory of Sarah Jessica Parker acolytes, there was the Cosmopolitan, created by bartender Toby Cecchini at the Odeon in New York City, in 1988. Adapted from a pink-hued mock-martini recipe that had been floating around Florida and San Francisco, Cecchini retooled the ingredient list with higher-quality mixers, choosing Citron vodka, Cointreau, lime juice, and cranberry juice. Despite common pop culture associations, the original Cosmopolitan is a rather dry cocktail, all the more so if you use natural, unsweetened cranberry juice in place of cranberry juice cocktail. The recipe can also be tweaked with other orange liqueurs such as Combier, which will result in a slightly sweeter profile

---

| 2 OUNCES CITRON VODKA, PREFERABLY ABSOLUT | 1 OUNCE COINTREAU

1 OUNCE LIME JUICE | ½ OUNCE CRANBERRY JUICE |

Add all ingredients to a cocktail shaker. Add ice and shake until chilled. Strain into a chilled coupe or cocktail glass.

DOROTHY'S DELIGHT

 SERVES 25

CAITLIN LAMAN, CHICAGO, IL

In her Dorothy's Delight (named for her grandmother), Caitlin Laman riffs on a base of two quintessential punch ingredients—tea and brandy. She combines them with coffee liqueur and dry oloroso sherry for a rich, smoky, and slightly bitter drink that's ideal for kicking off an evening. Be sure to drink the remainder of the oloroso as you are making the punch," says Laman.

---

24 OUNCES BRANDY, PREFERABLY TARIQUET VS ARMAGNAC

8 OUNCES OLOROSO SHERRY, PREFERABLY FERNANDO DE CASTILLA OLOROSO

2 OUNCES COFFEE LIQUEUR, PREFERABLY ST. GEORGE NOLA

3 OUNCES LEMON JUICE

14 OUNCES BREWED ROOIBOS TEA

10 OUNCES GRAPEFRUIT OLEO-SACCHARUM (SEE NOTE)

GARNISH
LEMON WHEELS

Combine all ingredients in a large container and let sit for 24 hours at room temperature. Strain into a punch bowl. Garnish with lemon wheels. Ladle into cups over ice.

NOTE To make the grapefruit oleo-saccharum, macerate 2 ounces grapefruit peel and 1 ounce lemon peel in 8 ounces sugar. Pour into a resealable plastic bag and squeeze out as much air as possible before sealing. Let sit for 24 hours. Remove peels before using.

FILIBUSTER

SERVES 1

ERIK ADKINS, SLANTED DOOR, SAN FRANCISCO, CA

San Francisco bartender Erik Adkins starts with the basic Whiskey Sour (page 198) blueprint for this autumn-inspired drink. Instead of using simple syrup, he substitutes Grade B maple syrup to create a deep, frothy cocktail topped with spicy Angostura bitters. The Filibuster throws a bit of heat thanks to its strong rye backbone; Adkins recommends using a lower-proof rye in order to preserve the foamy egg white. As for the name? "I found it in the horse racing pages," says Adkins. "Years ago, [drinks writer] Simon Difford joked that if you needed a name for a cocktail, check out the racing pages. I liked Filibuster because it sounded like it was a classic from a hundred years ago."

---

2 OUNCES RYE, PREFERABLY SAZERAC 6-YEAR

¾ OUNCE LEMON JUICE

½ OUNCE MAPLE SYRUP, GRADE B

½ OUNCE OR 1 SMALL EGG WHITE

GARNISH
ANGOSTURA BITTERS

Add all ingredients to a cocktail shaker and dry shake. Add ice and shake well. Strain into a chilled coupe or cocktail glass. To garnish, dash Angostura bitters around the perimeter of the drink and then drag a toothpick through them to create a garland of hearts.

FITTY-FITTY MARTINI

 | **SERVES 1** |

AUDREY SAUNDERS, PEGU CLUB, NEW YORK, NY

The martini spent the better part of the 1980s and 1990s as a stripped-down, mostly gin (or, gasp, vodka) version of itself. For some reason, it was cool to request just a whisper of vermouth. In an effort to reintroduce America to the joys of dry vermouth and orange bitters, Audrey Saunders created the sophisticated Fitty-Fitty cocktail at her New York City bar, Pegu Club. She calls the drink a true study in calibration, taking into account not only the botanical profile of the gin, but the vermouth, too: When she has Noilly Prat vermouth on hand, Saunders likes to match it with more assertive Tanqueray gin. However, if she's using the more delicate Dolin Dry vermouth, she'll team that up with more easygoing Plymouth. Even the bitters that Saunders uses are 50-50: a blend of Regan's and Fee Brothers. "The lemon twist is non-negotiable," says Saunders. "It simply isn't a Fitty-Fitty without it."

| 1½ OUNCES GIN

1½ OUNCES DRY VERMOUTH | 2 DASHES ORANGE BITTERS, PREFERABLY 1 EACH OF REGAN'S AND FEE BROTHERS | **GARNISH**
LEMON TWIST |

Add all ingredients to a mixing glass. Add ice and stir until chilled. Strain into a chilled coupe or cocktail glass. Garnish with a lemon twist.

FLANNEL SHIRT

 | **SERVES 1** |

JEFFREY MORGENTHALER, CLYDE COMMON, PORTLAND, OR

Bartender Jeffrey Morgenthaler created the Flannel Shirt using classic fall flavors—apple, earth, spice, and smoke—to imitate a mulled cider. The fleecy, bone-warming drink has a bold backbone of Scotch and a supporting cast of apple cider, St. Elizabeth Allspice Dram, and bittersweet Amaro Averna. Morgenthaler says, "It reminds me of a hot drink that you'd have on Thanksgiving morning—only served cold."

1¾ OUNCES SCOTCH

1½ OUNCES
APPLE CIDER

½ OUNCE
AMARO AVERNA

¼ OUNCE
LEMON JUICE

1 TEASPOON RICH
SIMPLE SYRUP
(PAGE 332)

½ TEASPOON
ST. ELIZABETH
ALLSPICE DRAM

2 DASHES ANGOSTURA
BITTERS

GARNISH
ORANGE PEEL

Add all ingredients to a cocktail shaker. Add ice and shake until chilled. Strain into a rocks glass over ice. Garnish with an orange peel.

FLATIRON MARTINI

 **SERVES 1**

JULIE REINER, FLATIRON LOUNGE, NEW YORK, NY

When Julie Reiner first opened her Flatiron Lounge in Manhattan in 2003, flavorless vodka was still the booze of choice among bar-goers, which meant that a gin martini wasn't going to fly. Reiner made this 50/50 martini, a vodka–Lillet Blanc split, the bar's trademark drink. The Lillet gives the drink an impressive aromatic presence and touch of sweetness that the usual dry vermouth doesn't have. Reiner is constantly tinkering with her own drinks; in recent years, she has updated this martini by using Cocchi Americano Bianco instead of Lillet for a more bitter edge.

¼ OUNCE COINTREAU

1½ OUNCES VODKA

1½ OUNCES
LILLET BLANC

GARNISH
ORANGE PEEL

Rinse a cocktail glass with Cointreau and throw out excess Cointreau. In a mixing glass filled with ice, combine vodka and Lillet and stir until chilled. Strain into the prepared glass and garnish with an orange peel.

FROZEN NEGRONI

 | **SERVES 1** |

JEFFREY MORGENTHALER, CLYDE COMMON, PORTLAND, OR

Jeffrey Morgenthaler's Frozen Negroni began as a Negroni sno-cone he used to serve at backyard dinners. He has tinkered with the ratios a little over time, but doesn't stray too far from tradition: Campari, gin, and sweet vermouth, along with simple syrup and lots of ice. When slushifying cocktails, Morgenthaler tends to add some fruit juice to the equation. "It adds body and dilutes with flavor rather than just water," he says. "Consider the cocktail and pick the juice accordingly." He recommends trying grapefruit juice in a martini and pomegranate juice in a Manhattan, and suggests plastic Solo cups as the most appropriate serving vessel.

1 OUNCE CAMPARI

1 OUNCE GIN

1 OUNCE SWEET VERMOUTH

¾ OUNCE SIMPLE SYRUP (PAGE 332)

JUICE OF 1 ORANGE

GARNISH
ORANGE SLICE

Add all ingredients to a blender. Add ice (Morgenthaler suggests starting with 6 ounces, adding more if necessary). Blend until smooth. Pour into a plastic cup or rocks glass and garnish with an orange slice.

GIN AND JUICE

 SERVES 1

JADE SOTACK, NEW YORK, NY

At Wassail, New York City's fantastic Lower East Side cider bar, cider cocktails are a mainstay. Former bartender Jade Sotack came up with several seasonal iterations of what she calls Gin and Juice. For this springtime version, a play on a Gin and Tonic (page 95), Sotack combines a concentrated tonic syrup and just ½ ounce of gin to provide the base flavors, then top the whole thing off with a *sidra* (cider) from Spain's Asturias for a funkier version of the classic refresher—but any high-acid cider will work here. This drink takes on a completely different personality depending on which gin you use. Sotack is partial to both Tanqueray and Hayman's Old Tom.

½ OUNCE GIN	4 OUNCES SPANISH *SIDRA*, PREFERABLY TRABANCO	**GARNISH** LEMON PEEL
1 OUNCE TONIC SYRUP, PREFERABLY SMALL HAND FOODS		

Add all ingredients to an ice-filled double rocks or Collins glass, and stir to combine. Garnish with a lemon peel.

GIN BLOSSOM

 **SERVES 1**

JULIE REINER, CLOVER CLUB, BROOKLYN, NY

Bartender Julie Reiner devised a signature Martini for each of her NYC bars; the Gin Blossom is the staple at Clover Club, in Brooklyn. A more aromatic take on the original, it mashes up fruity apricot eau-de-vie with the floral, vanilla notes of Martini & Rossi Bianco and the herbaceous profile of gin. For a drier, more bitter version, Reiner recommends using Contratto Bianco—bitter, orange-tinged bianco vermouth from Torino.

1½ OUNCES BOMBAY DRY GIN	¾ OUNCE APRICOT EAU-DE-VIE	**GARNISH** ORANGE PEEL
1½ OUNCES MARTINI & ROSSI BIANCO	2 DASHES ORANGE BITTERS	

Add all ingredients to a mixing glass. Add ice and stir to chill. Strain into a coupe glass and garnish with an expressed (twisted over top to release fragrant oils) orange peel.

GLASGOW MULE

 | **SERVES 1** |

DAMON BOELTE, GRAND ARMY BAR, BROOKLYN, NY

Named for its Scotch foundation, the Glasgow Mule is Brooklyn bartender Damon Boelte's take on the simple mule formula: spirit, citrus, ginger beer. It's a neat example of how swapping out a base spirit can completely change the intention and balance of a cocktail. The intensity of the Scotch requires a little extra reinforcement, so Boelte built upon it with fresh lemon, versatile St-Germain elderflower liqueur, and spicy Fever Tree ginger beer, plus a dash of aromatic Angostura bitters to complete this tart and spicy cocktail.

1½ OUNCES BLENDED SCOTCH

½ OUNCE ST-GERMAIN

¾ OUNCE LEMON JUICE

1 DASH ANGOSTURA BITTERS

4 OUNCES GINGER BEER, PREFERABLY FEVER TREE

GARNISH
LEMON WHEEL AND CANDIED GINGER ON A PICK

Build all ingredients in a large mule mug (if you're the sort who owns one) or a Collins glass. Add crushed ice and stir. Garnish with a lemon wheel and candied ginger on a pick.

GO-TO

SERVES 1

ROB KRUEGER, EXTRA FANCY, BROOKLYN, NY

"Ginger beer has been called ketchup," says Rob Krueger, meaning that it's a dependably crowd-pleasing ingredient in the cocktail world. But that doesn't make it any less delicious. Here, Krueger puts it alongside gin, cucumber, mint, and St-Germain—the original bartender's ketchup. Variations on this drink have long been Krueger's answer to requests for a refreshing gin or vodka drink that's not too sweet or might have cucumber, etc. He mentioned this to a guest one night, to which she responded, "Oh, so it's your go-to?" inspiring the cocktail's name.

2 OUNCES GIN, PREFERABLY FORD'S	3 CUCUMBER SLICES	**GARNISH** MINT SPRIG AND CUCUMBER WHEELS
½ OUNCE ST-GERMAIN	8-10 MINT LEAVES	
¾ OUNCE LIME JUICE	GINGER BEER, TO TOP	

Combine gin, St-Germain, and lime juice in a Collins glass. Add ice, then top with cucumber slices and mint. "Cheat shake" by capping the glass with a small mixing tin and shaking briefly. Top with ginger beer. Garnish with fresh mint and cucumber wheels.

HEART-SHAPED BOX

| SERVES 1 |

FREDDY SCHWENK, CHAUHAN ALE AND MASALA HOUSE, NASHVILLE, TN

Whereas the traditional Pimm's Cup (page 152) is made with fruit-forward, low-proof Pimm's No. 1, Freddy Schwenk punches up this heady, modern variation with lemongrass, bitter lemon soda, and some extra gin for good measure, cutting the sweetness of the drink with a squeeze of lime. Even though the cocktail's color evokes Valentine's Day, its name was actually inspired by a Nirvana song.

HANDFUL OF RASPBERRIES

2 CUCUMBER SLICES

1½ OUNCES PIMM'S NO. 1

½ OUNCE GIN, PREFERABLY RANSOM OLD TOM

¼ OUNCE LIME JUICE

¼ OUNCE LEMONGRASS SYRUP (SEE NOTE)

BITTER LEMON SODA, PREFERABLY FEVER TREE, TO TOP

GARNISH
FRESH RASPBERRIES ON A BAMBOO SKEWER

In a mixing tin, muddle raspberries and cucumber slices. Add Pimm's, gin, lime juice, and lemongrass syrup. Shake, then double strain into a tall Collins glass. Top with lemon soda. Garnish with raspberries on a bamboo skewer.

NOTE To make lemongrass syrup, combine 1 part water, 1 part sugar, and 4 lemongrass stalks in a saucepan over medium heat. Bring to a boil and remove from heat. Let cool for 2 hours, then strain out lemongrass. Will keep, refrigerated, for 1 month.

HIBISCUS PUNCH ROYALE

 | **SERVES 12** |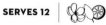

MARTIN CATE, SMUGGLER'S COVE AND WHITECHAPEL, SAN FRANCISCO, CA

A riff on Smuggler's Cove's ever-popular Hibiscus Rum Punch (the bar sells a hundred of these drinks a week)—which is itself a riff on the Caribbean classic Spiced Hibiscus Punch—this large-format holiday recipe from Martin Cate combines aged rum and fresh lime with tart hibiscus syrup. Add a hefty pour of chilled cava and preserved Jamaican hibiscus flowers, and you've got a prime party starter based on looks alone.

18 OUNCES BLENDED AGED RUM, PREFERABLY APPLETON ESTATE RESERVE BLEND

12 OUNCES HIBISCUS SYRUP (SEE NOTE)

4 OUNCES RICH SIMPLE SYRUP (PAGE 332)

6 OUNCES LIME JUICE

24 OUNCES CAVA, CHILLED

GARNISH
HIBISCUS FLOWERS IN SYRUP (DRAINED), LIME WHEELS, AND MINT SPRIGS

Combine all ingredients, except cava, and chill for 2 hours. Twenty minutes before serving, add chilled ingredients to punch bowl filled with cracked ice. Top with cava and stir gently to combine. Garnish bowl with hibiscus flowers resting on lime wheels, and mint sprigs.

NOTE To make hibiscus syrup, add 1 cup water, 1 cup hibiscus blossoms, and a lemon peel to a pot and bring to a boil. Add 1 cup sugar and stir to dissolve. Turn off heat and allow to cool before storing in the refrigerator in an airtight container. Will keep, refrigerated, for 1 month.

HOP OVER

SERVES 1

TOM RICHTER, DEAR IRVING, NEW YORK, NY

When bartender Tom Richter was looking to create a new beer cocktail, he built on the classic radler template starting with a hoppy IPA as the bitter, aromatic foundation. "I just kept adding components that I thought would fill out the balance," he says. This meant malty genever (gin's OG predecessor) to complement the beer, with the fitting additions of sweet-spicy falernum and orange flower water.

½ OUNCE LEMON JUICE

¾ OUNCE VELVET FALERNUM

1 OUNCE GENEVER

2 DASHES ORANGE FLOWER WATER

HOPPY IPA, TO TOP

GARNISH
LEMON WHEELS

Combine all ingredients in a pint glass over cracked ice and top with beer. Garnish with lemon wheels.

ITALIAN BUCK

 **SERVES 1**

JAMIE BOUDREAU, CANON, SEATTLE, WA

The essential ingredient in a buck is ginger ale or ginger beer. From there, just add a spirit, some citrus, and perhaps a dash of bitters. In the case of Jamie Boudreau's Italian Buck, the additions are, appropriately, all Italian. The Seattle bartender mixes Italian artichoke-based Cynar with the Bolognese Amaro Montenegro and fresh lime juice for a sprightly, bittersweet long cocktail for all seasons.

1½ OUNCES CYNAR

1½ OUNCES AMARO MONTENEGRO

¾ OUNCE LIME JUICE

3 OUNCES GINGER BEER

GARNISH LIME WHEELS

To a cocktail shaker, add Cynar, Amaro Montenegro, and lime juice. Add ice and shake until chilled. Strain into a Collins glass over ice. Top up with ginger beer and more ice, if necessary. Garnish with lime wheels.

JOGGLING BOARD

 | **SERVES 1**

GREG BEST, TICONDEROGA CLUB, ATLANTA, GA

With a base of white rum, the Joggling Board is a dressed-up riff on the Daiquiri (page 74) named for a piece of furniture hailing from South Carolina's Low Country: a joggling board is an extra-long bench grounded with rocking chair–style skiffs so it flexes and bounces, or "joggles," its sitters as they rock. Says bartender Greg Best, "Balancing flavors is very much like creating a plate of food. The Lillet rosé really brings a softening floral fragrance with perfect weight and viscosity to the blend, allowing me to weave the other ingredients together while rounding the harder edges from the ginger and rum."

1 OUNCE WHITE RUM, PREFERABLY DENIZEN	½ OUNCE GRAPEFRUIT JUICE	1 PINCH FRESH-CRACKED BLACK PEPPER
½ OUNCE ORANGE CURAÇAO, PREFERABLY PIERRE FERRAND	¼ OUNCE KING'S GINGER LIQUEUR	1 DASH ANGOSTURA BITTERS
½ OUNCE LILLET ROSÉ	¼ OUNCE LEMON JUICE	**GARNISH** PINCH OF SEA SALT

Add all ingredients to a cocktail shaker. Add ice and shake until chilled. Strain into a chilled coupe or cocktail glass. Garnish with a pinch of sea salt.

KENTUCKY BUCK

 | **SERVES 1** |

ERICK CASTRO, POLITE PROVISIONS, SAN DIEGO, CA

Named for Kentucky's state spirit—bourbon, of course—and with the addition of muddled strawberry and fresh lemon, Erick Castro's Southern rendition of a traditional buck couldn't be better suited to a long, lazy afternoon.

---

1 STRAWBERRY	¾ OUNCE LEMON JUICE	GINGER BEER, TO TOP
½ OUNCE SIMPLE SYRUP (PAGE 332)	2 DASHES ANGOSTURA BITTERS	**GARNISH** LEMON WHEEL
2 OUNCES BOURBON		

In a cocktail shaker, muddle strawberry with simple syrup. Add bourbon, lemon juice, bitters, and ice and shake until chilled. Double strain into a Collins glass over ice and top with ginger beer. Garnish with a lemon wheel.

LA BOMBA DAIQUIRI

SERVES 1

JOAQUÍN SIMÓ, POURING RIBBONS, NEW YORK, NY

Joaquín Simó's riff on the Daiquiri (page 74) derives its name from the word for "bomb" in Spanish, but it also winks at the French word *grenade*, meaning "pomegranate"—an ingredient that plays an important role in this drink. Here, pomegranate molasses lends a complex tanginess that gives depth to tart fresh raspberries and vibrant lime juice. "This cocktail is an awesome way to prove that 'fruity' and 'sweet' are not synonymous," says Simó.

---

5 RASPBERRIES

½ OUNCE SIMPLE
SYRUP (PAGE 332)

2 OUNCES WHITE RUM

¾ OUNCE LIME JUICE

1 TEASPOON
POMEGRANATE
MOLASSES

GARNISH
LIME AND
RASPBERRY SKEWER

In a cocktail shaker, muddle raspberries with simple syrup. Add remaining ingredients and ice, and shake until chilled. Double strain into a chilled coupe or cocktail glass. Garnish with a lime and raspberry skewer.

LATIN TRIFECTA

 **SERVES 1**

JAMIE BOUDREAU, CANON, SEATTLE, WA

Drawing on ingredients from romance language–speaking countries, the Latin Trifecta honors Mexico, Italy, and Spain with the strong and savory trio of tequila, Cynar, and sherry. About his creation, Jamie Boudreau says, "Tequila and sherry have always been great friends; adding the bittersweet complexity of an amaro elevates the pairing." Indeed, the three form a perfect trio.

1 OUNCE TEQUILA	½ OUNCE DRY SHERRY (OLOROSO)	**GARNISH** FLAMED ORANGE PEEL (SEE PAGE 28)
1 OUNCE CYNAR	3 DASHES ORANGE BITTERS	

Add all ingredients to a mixing glass. Add ice and stir until chilled. Strain into a chilled coupe or cocktail glass. Garnish with a flamed orange peel.

LEFTY'S FIZZ

 | **SERVES 1** |

RYAN FITZGERALD, ABV, SAN FRANCISCO, CA

A menu staple at San Francisco's ABV, this drink was inspired by a single mezcal and named for the man who makes it: Del Maguey's Santo Domingo Albarradas, and *mezcalero* Espiridion "Lefty" Morales Luis. The smoky, single-village bottling reminded bartender Ryan Fitzgerald of maraschino liqueur, and using that as a launchpad he called on the flavors of a Hemingway Daiquiri (page 105), in which maraschino also plays an important role. The mezcal gets mixed with sweet-and-sour grapefruit shrub, lime juice, dry curaçao, and egg white. Served down over soda water, the fluffed-up fizz is equal parts sour, smoky, and smooth.

---

2 OUNCES SODA WATER	½ OUNCE DRY CURAÇAO, PREFERABLY PIERRE FERRAND	1 EGG WHITE
1½ OUNCES DEL MAGUEY SANTO DOMINGO ALBARRADAS MEZCAL (NO SUBSTITUTE)	¾ OUNCE LIME JUICE	**GARNISH** GRAPEFRUIT PEEL
	¾ OUNCE SHRUB & CO. GRAPEFRUIT SHRUB	

Add soda water to a rocks glass. Add remaining ingredients to a cocktail shaker. Dry shake. Add ice and shake until chilled. Strain over soda water into glass. Garnish with a grapefruit peel.

LONG ISLAND BAR GIMLET

 | **SERVES 1** |

TOBY CECCHINI, LONG ISLAND BAR, BROOKLYN, NY

Eschewing the traditional Rose's Lime Cordial, Brooklyn bartender Toby Cecchini doubles down on the lime in his super-tangy gimlet, using both a house-made ginger-infused lime cordial and an extra dose of fresh lime juice. The cordial requires time and resolve, but you won't regret it.

2 OUNCES GIN	1 OUNCE LIME-GINGER CORDIAL (SEE NOTE)	**GARNISH** 2 LIME WHEELS
	¾ OUNCE LIME JUICE	

Add all ingredients to a cocktail shaker. Add ice and shake until chilled. Strain over ice into a rocks glass. Garnish with lime wheels.

NOTE To make lime-ginger cordial, peel 9 limes and reserve the fruit. Add the peels to a plastic container and cover with 1½ cups sugar, mixing to fully cover the peels. Leave at room temperature overnight. Meanwhile, juice the peeled limes. Peel ½ pound of fresh ginger and cut into 1-inch pieces. Add lime juice and ginger to a blender and pulse until well-combined. The next morning, pour this mixture over the lime-sugar mixture and stir until well incorporated. Let rest again at room temperature for 24 hours. Strain, discarding the solids. Pour into an airtight container and refrigerate for 24 hours before using. Makes about 1 quart of cordial.

MEXICAN TRICYCLE

 | **SERVES 1** |

ANDREW VOLK, PORTLAND HUNT & ALPINE CLUB, PORTLAND, ME

The classic Bicicletta (page 48) template, equal parts Campari and dry white wine topped up with soda water, is, like its sister the Spritz, endlessly riffable. At Maine's Portland Hunt & Alpine Club, bartender Andrew Volk has created several versions, including the White Noise (made with Cocchi Americano and elderflower liqueur), which he keeps on tap, and this, the Mexican Tricycle, his cool-weather iteration. Here, smoky mezcal acts as the backbone of the drink, standing up to the sweetness of the cider with an added kick of bitter Cynar, making for a simple, refreshing, and low-proof cocktail.

1 OUNCE MEZCAL, PREFERABLY DEL MAGUEY VIDA 1 OUNCE CYNAR	HARD CIDER, PREFERABLY BANTAM WUNDERKIND OR ANOTHER LIGHTLY SWEET CRAFT CIDER, TO TOP	**GARNISH** LIME WHEEL

Add mezcal and Cynar to a 10-ounce Collins glass. Fill with ice and top up with cider. Garnish with a lime wheel.

MOTT AND MULBERRY

 | **SERVES 1** |

LEO ROBITSCHEK, THE NOMAD BAR, NEW YORK, NY

Named for two streets in New York City's Little Italy, the Mott and Mulberry is bartender Leo Robitschek's autumnal riff on a Whiskey Sour (page 198)—a balance of Italian and American ingredients. "My original idea was to create a cold version of a mulled cider that could be drunk year-round," he says. His mix of spicy rye, peppery Amaro Abano, and tart apple cider layered over rich Demerara syrup and fresh lemon combine to make a bone-warming drink.

1 OUNCE RYE, PREFERABLY OLD OVERHOLT	¾ OUNCE APPLE CIDER OR TART APPLE JUICE	½ OUNCE DEMERARA SYRUP (PAGE 332)
1 OUNCE LUXARDO AMARO ABANO	½ OUNCE LEMON JUICE	**GARNISH** THIN APPLE SLICES

Add all ingredients to a cocktail shaker. Add ice and shake until chilled. Strain into a rocks glass over ice. Garnish with thinly sliced apple.

MOUNTAIN MAN

 **SERVES 1**

NATASHA DAVID, NITECAP, NEW YORK, NY

In this kicked-up Whiskey Sour (the original appears on page 193), Natasha David calls for maple syrup as the sweetener. "It adds an entirely different flavor than regular simple syrup or even a rich sugar like Demerara." David forgoes fresh peaches in lieu of Giffard's Pêche de Vigne to accentuate the roundness of the maple syrup and the spicy ginger. "A lot of other fruit liqueurs can taste artificial," she says. "But I find that Giffard is always a very true expression of each fruit."

2 OUNCES BOURBON, PREFERABLY OLD FORESTER

¼ OUNCE GIFFARD PÊCHE DE VIGNE

¾ OUNCE LEMON JUICE

¼ OUNCE MAPLE SYRUP

¼ OUNCE GINGER SYRUP (PAGE 333)

GARNISH
CANDIED GINGER

Add all ingredients to a cocktail shaker. Add ice and shake until chilled. Strain over a large ice cube into a rocks glass. Garnish with a piece or two of candied ginger.

NATOMA ST.

 | **SERVES 1** |

CAITLIN LAMAN, CHICAGO, IL

"My manager at a not-to-be-named restaurant I worked at years ago asked for something Negroni-like that wouldn't knock him on his ass—something he could continue to drink all shift long," says bartender Caitlin Laman. Her response: a low-proof riff on a Negroni (page 135) consisting of sherry and bitter-yet-rich Gran Classico, balanced out with dry vermouth. Laman describes this as a "refreshing, herbal, bitter, sherry-driven cocktail that you can drink all night long." Amen.

| 1 OUNCE AMONTILLADO SHERRY, PREFERABLY HIDALGO NAPOLEON | 1 OUNCE GRAN CLASSICO BITTER

1 OUNCE DRY VERMOUTH, PREFERABLY DOLIN | **GARNISH** LEMON PEEL |

Add all ingredients to a mixing glass with ice and stir. Strain into a rocks glass with one large ice cube. Garnish with a lemon peel.

OAXACA OLD-FASHIONED

 | **SERVES 1** |

PHILIP WARD, MAYAHUEL, NEW YORK, NY

Philip Ward devised this smoky take on the Old-Fashioned nearly a decade ago, back when he was behind the bar at NYC's Death & Co. "I was just starting to play with mezcal in cocktails and noticed that adding a bit of mezcal to tequila drinks was like putting your tequila on steroids. More body, more smoke, more everything you ever dreamed tequila could be," he says. To balance the big flavor of mezcal, Ward uses agave nectar because it's a little richer than simple syrup. And while his go-to bitters are Angostura, he'll often swap them for molé bitters to bring a little extra Mexican flavor.

1½ OUNCES EL TESORO
REPOSADO TEQUILA

½ OUNCE DEL MAGUEY
SAN LUIS DEL RIO
MEZCAL

2 DASHES ANGOSTURA
BITTERS

1 BARSPOON
AGAVE NECTAR

GARNISH
FLAMED ORANGE
PEEL (SEE PAGE 28)

Combine all the ingredients in an old-fashioned glass with one large ice cube. Stir until chilled. Top with a flamed orange peel.

OLD HICKORY

 | **SERVES 1** |

MAXWELL BRITTEN, BROOKLYN, NY

"I like to pay homage to the lesser known New Orleans cocktails," says Maxwell Britten. He adapted his Old Hickory—a reference to President Andrew Jackson's nickname—from Stanley Clisby Arthur's 1937 *Famous New Orleans Drinks and How to Mix 'Em*. Britten's version includes the addition of Peychaud's bitters, another nod to the drink's New Orleans roots. Because Old Hickory is a vermouth-based, low-proof cocktail, Britten likes to suggest it as an unorthodox but compatible companion to oysters.

1½ OUNCES SWEET VERMOUTH, PREFERABLY CARPANO ANTICA	1 OUNCE DRY VERMOUTH, PREFERABLY DOLIN	4 DASHES ORANGE BITTERS
	4 DASHES PEYCHAUD'S BITTERS	**GARNISH** ORANGE PEEL

Add all ingredients to a mixing glass. Add ice and stir until chilled. Strain over ice into a rocks glass. Garnish with an orange peel.

OXFORD COMMA

 **SERVES 1**

JEREMY OERTEL, DONNA, BROOKLYN, NY

On a mission to create a new gin drink for Brooklyn bar Dram, bartender Jeremy Oertel took inspiration from a bizarre source: one of his favorite drinks from the New York *tequila* bar Mayahuel. "I wanted to find a way to combine the flavors of a shaken cocktail—called the Loop Tonic—into a stirred cocktail," says Oertel. "I liked the way that celery and green Chartreuse go together, so I maintained those flavors and added maraschino for a hint of sweetness." He didn't have a name for it, so he turned it over to Dram's owner, Tom Chadwick, who went back to his office to print menus. "My guess is, Tom was probably listing the ingredients and used an Oxford comma to separate the final components. He's a funny guy like that," Oertel says.

---

2 OUNCES GIN, PREFERABLY PLYMOUTH

¾ OUNCE DRY VERMOUTH

½ OUNCE GREEN CHARTREUSE

1 TEASPOON MARASCHINO LIQUEUR

1 DASH BITTERMENS ORCHARD STREET CELERY SHRUB

GARNISH LEMON PEEL

Add all ingredients to a mixing glass. Add ice and stir until chilled. Strain into a chilled coupe or cocktail glass. Garnish with a lemon peel.

PADANG SWIZZLE

 **SERVES 1**

ZAC OVERMAN, L'OURSIN, SEATTLE, WA

Most tiki drinks are born of visions of palm trees and orchid leis, but Zac Overman's Padang Swizzle (named for the capital of West Sumatra, Indonesia) was conceived in the dead of winter in Brooklyn's wind-whipped Red Hook neighborhood. In an attempt to tiki-fy the Sherry Cobbler (page 173), he added rum and smoky Islay Scotch, which mimics the aroma coming off the burning cinnamon stick garnish. "The end result is a rich, nutty, warmly spiced yet refreshing cocktail that both tastes smoky and is literally smoking," he says.

1½ OUNCES AMONTILLADO SHERRY, PREFERABLY LUSTAU LOS ARCOS

½ OUNCE AGED RUM, PREFERABLY ENGLISH HARBOUR 5-YEAR

¼ OUNCE ISLAY SINGLE-MALT SCOTCH, PREFERABLY LAPHROAIG 10-YEAR

¾ OUNCE LIME JUICE

½ OUNCE GRAPEFRUIT JUICE

¾ OUNCE CINNAMON SYRUP (PAGE 333)

GARNISH
SMOKING CINNAMON STICK AND A LIME WHEEL

Add all ingredients to a Collins or pilsner glass. Add crushed ice and swizzle using a swizzle stick or barspoon. Top with more crushed ice, and garnish with a lime wheel speared through with a smoking cinnamon stick (carefully light using a match or lighter). Be sure to extinguish the cinnamon stick before attempting to take a sip of your swizzle.

PAPER PLANE

 | **SERVES 1**

SAM ROSS, ATTABOY, NEW YORK, NY

During his time behind the stick at NYC's infamous Milk & Honey, bartender Sam Ross created several drinks that have become keystones of the cocktail revolution; the Paper Plane is one. Ross claims that that he devised it while listening to British rapper MIA's song of the same name, but it's inconceivable that he could have whipped up a cocktail this balanced, with such boisterous ingredients, with any sort of diversion. The drink combines four ingredients in equal measure, which at first glance seems like the easy way out, but somehow, each element is bolder than the last.

¾ OUNCE BOURBON

¾ OUNCE AMARO NONINO QUINTESSENTIA

¾ OUNCE APEROL

¾ OUNCE FRESH LEMON JUICE

Combine all ingredients in a cocktail shaker three-quarters filled with ice. Shake until chilled. Strain into a coupe.

PARISH HALL PUNCH

 **SERVES 8**

DAMON BOELTE, GRAND ARMY BAR, BROOKLYN, NY

Childhood memories of post–church service punch bowls filled with ginger ale and garishly colored sweet sherbet in the parish hall are what spurred Oklahoma native Damon Boelte to create this punch. This more sophisticated—and boozy—adult version improbably replicates the classic flavors.

2 GRAPEFRUITS

¼ CUP SUGAR

½ CUP OLD TOM GIN, PREFERABLY GREENHOOK GINSMITHS' OR HAYMAN'S OLD TOM

½ CUP AMONTILLADO SHERRY

½ CUP BASQUE CIDER, PREFERABLY ISASTEGI

½ CUP GINGER BEER, PREFERABLY FEVER TREE

¼ CUP SELTZER WATER

GARNISH
1 (3-INCH) KNOB FRESH GINGER, PEELED AND CUT INTO COINS, GRAPEFRUIT SLICES

Peel grapefruits, taking care to avoid as much bitter white pith as possible. In a large bowl, combine sugar with grapefruit peels, then lightly muddle and let sit for 20 minutes to allow oils to infuse with sugar. After 20 minutes, add gin, sherry, cider, ginger beer, and seltzer. Stir to combine. Add ginger and grapefruit slices to the bowl to garnish. To serve, ladle into punch cups over ice.

PENICILLIN

 | **SERVES 1** |

SAM ROSS, ATTABOY, NEW YORK, NY

Sam Ross's creation of the Penicillin cocktail as one of modern drinking's first cult faves was nearly as groundbreaking as the discovery of penicillin as one of modern medicine's first antibiotics. The Penicillin has been made in bars around the world since Ross first served it at New York's venerated Milk & Honey in 2007. The soothing tonic of honey, lemon, and ginger is bolstered by two layers of Scotch, a pleasant cure for whatever ails you.

---

2 OUNCES BLENDED
SCOTCH, SUCH AS
FAMOUS GROUSE

¾ OUNCE HONEY-
GINGER SYRUP
(SEE NOTE)

¾ OUNCE FRESH
LEMON JUICE

¼ OUNCE ISLAY
SINGLE-MALT
SCOTCH, PREFERABLY
LAPHROAIG 10-YEAR

GARNISH
CANDIED GINGER

Combine blended Scotch with honey-ginger syrup and lemon juice in a cocktail shaker three-quarters filled with ice. Shake until chilled. Strain into a rocks glass filled with one large ice cube. Top with Islay Scotch and garnish with candied ginger.

NOTE To make honey-ginger syrup, combine 1 cup honey with one 6-inch peeled and sliced piece ginger root and 1 cup water in a small pot and bring to a boil. Lower heat and simmer for 5 minutes. Refrigerate overnight, then strain and discard solids.

PIÑA VERDE

SERVES 1

ERICK CASTRO, POLITE PROVISIONS, SAN DIEGO, CA

Playfully dubbed the "Green-Yuh Colada" by the staff at Polite Provisions, the Piña Verde was originally inspired by Erick Castro's unorthodox addition of a green Chartreuse float to his piña coladas years ago. His aim was to create a rich drink with herbaceous flavor. When rum—and then later gin—didn't cut it, Castro ditched the spirit altogether and upped the liqueur to pick up the slack. "At 55 percent ABV, this allowed the liqueur to stretch out its wings and really claim ownership of the cocktail," he says. Pineapple juice and lime add a fruity kick, while the piña colada staple, Coco Lopez, keeps it tethered to the original.

1½ OUNCES GREEN CHARTREUSE	¾ OUNCE COCO LOPEZ CREAM OF COCONUT	**GARNISH** MINT SPRIG
1½ OUNCES PINEAPPLE JUICE	½ OUNCE LIME JUICE	

Add all ingredients to a blender and add ice (5 or 6 regular-size cubes, cracked). Blend until smooth, and pour into a tiki mug. Garnish with a mint sprig.

NOTE Start with just a little ice and add more as you blend until you've achieved your preferred texture.

POMPELMO SOUR

 **SERVES 1**

SARAH BOISJOLI, NEW YORK, NY

Equal parts grapefruit sour and lemon milk shake, Sarah Boisjoli's Pompelmo Sour from New York's Estela uses a grapefruit oleo-saccharum to create a deep citrusy base. This old-school method of infusing sugar with citrus oils was initially used for making punches in the nineteenth century, but bartenders today are using it in many applications. "There's a higher extraction of flavor and a lower amount of dilution when we use a syrup like this versus simple syrup and grapefruit juice," says Boisjoli.

1½ OUNCES GIN, PREFERABLY NEW YORK DISTILLING COMPANY'S DOROTHY PARKER

½ OUNCE AMARO MONTENEGRO

¾ OUNCE LEMON JUICE

½ OUNCE GRAPEFRUIT OLEO-SACCHARUM (SEE NOTE)

1 EGG WHITE

2 DASHES ANGOSTURA BITTERS

GARNISH
GRAPEFRUIT PEEL

Add all ingredients to a cocktail shaker. Dry shake. Add ice and shake until chilled. Strain into a chilled coupe or cocktail glass. Garnish with a grapefruit peel.

NOTE To make grapefruit oleo-saccharum, remove peel from 1 large grapefruit and chop peel roughly. Combine peel with 2 cups sugar and pack tightly into a container. Let mixture sit for 24 hours. Once infused, add 1½ cups cold or room temperature water to mixture and allow to dissolve. Strain, and discard solids.

POPPA'S PRIDE

SERVES 1

JAY ZIMMERMAN, BA'SIK, BROOKLYN, NY

A composite of a buck and a Whiskey Smash (page 197), this ginger-laced bourbon drink is one of Brooklyn bartender Jay Zimmerman's signatures. Instead of muddling the lemon wedges and mint leaves, he shakes the hell out of them along with a mix of bourbon and ginger juice and tops the drink with soda and Angostura bitters.

2 OUNCES BOURBON	2 LEMON WEDGES	4–5 DASHES ANGOSTURA BITTERS
1 OUNCE SWEETENED GINGER JUICE (SEE NOTE)	5 MINT LEAVES	
	2 OUNCES SODA WATER	**GARNISH** MINT SPRIG

Add bourbon, ginger juice, lemon wedges, and mint to a cocktail shaker. Add ice and shake until chilled. Strain into a highball or Collins glass over fresh ice. Top with soda water and Angostura bitters (don't be shy about the bitters). Garnish with a mint sprig.

NOTE Zimmerman uses 3 parts ginger juice to 1 part sugar for his sweetened ginger juice recipe. If you don't have access to fresh ginger juice, you can peel and chop a 2-inch cube of fresh ginger and muddle well with ¾ ounce simple syrup (page 332) in the bottom of a cocktail shaker before adding remaining ingredients.

RED HOOK

 | **SERVES 1**

VINCENZO ERRICO

This boozy cross between the Brooklyn (page 60) and the Manhattan (page 114) is the handiwork of former Milk & Honey bartender Vincenzo Errico. The drink, created in 2003, builds on the Manhattan and the Brooklyn's classic whiskey base, doses it with the subtly bitter, cherry-scented Italian vermouth Punt e Mes, and sweetens it up with the addition of maraschino liqueur. While there are a number of modern drinks that have played off the classic compositions of both the Manhattan and the Brooklyn, Errico's is one of the more enduring modern riffs.

| 2 OUNCES RYE | ½ OUNCE PUNT E MES | ¼ – ½ OUNCE MARASCHINO LIQUEUR, TO TASTE |

Add all ingredients to a mixing glass. Add ice and stir. Strain into a coupe or cocktail glass.

REVOLVER

 | **SERVES 1** |

JON SANTER, PRIZEFIGHTER, EMERYVILLE, CA

When Bulleit Bourbon first launched in 2004, it went off like a shot through the bartender cadre. Jon Santer was an early gunslinger, favoring the bourbon for its dry profile and perfectly high ABV. A big fan of St. George Spirits NOLA Coffee Liqueur, too, Santer found the Bulleit to be its perfect match in this dark drink. To finish it off, he flames an orange peel over the glass—both for a theatrical effect he loves at the bar, as well as for the smoky nose it gives the cocktail.

2 OUNCES BOURBON, PREFERABLY BULLEIT	½ OUNCE COFFEE LIQUEUR, PREFERABLY ST. GEORGE NOLA	**GARNISH** FLAMED ORANGE PEEL (SEE PAGE 28)
	2 DASHES ORANGE BITTERS	

Combine all ingredients in a mixing glass. Add ice and stir until chilled. Strain into a chilled coupe or cocktail glass. Garnish with a flamed orange peel.

RHYTHM AND SOUL

 | **SERVES 1** |

GREG BEST, TICONDEROGA CLUB, ATLANTA, GA

The Rhythm and Soul is Greg Best's composite sketch of a
Manhattan (page 114) and a Sazerac (page 168). "I imagine the two
cocktails getting into a tussle on the high street of a small frontier
town," says Best, "and then making up and having a love child."
With a base of bourbon and sweet vermouth, accented by the
licorice fragrance of Herbsaint, and balanced out with Averna and
Angostura bitters, this drink has, as Best says, "the rhythm of
a Manhattan and the soul of a Sazerac."

1 BARSPOON HERBSAINT	½ OUNCE SWEET VERMOUTH, PREFERABLY CARPANO ANTICA	4 DASHES ANGOSTURA BITTERS
1½ OUNCES BOURBON, PREFERABLY WATHEN'S	½ OUNCE AVERNA	**GARNISH** LEMON PEEL

Fill a rocks glass with cracked ice and add Herbsaint. Set aside. Add
remaining ingredients to a mixing glass. Add ice and stir until chilled.
Roll Herbsaint and ice mixture around the rocks glass to coat. Discard.
Strain contents of the mixing glass into the prepared glass. Garnish
with a lemon peel.

ROME WITH A VIEW

 **SERVES 1**

MICHAEL MCILROY, ATTABOY, NEW YORK, NY

Michael McIlroy's Rome with a View falls somewhere between a day drinking-appropriate Collins and an Americano (page 38). Whereas an Americano is built with bitter Italian Campari and sweet vermouth, McIlroy swaps in dry vermouth, and takes cues from the spirit-citrus-sweetener-soda formula of a Collins. Low-alcohol and bracingly bittersweet, it conjures warm afternoons looking out over an ancient Italian city.

1 OUNCE CAMPARI	1 OUNCE LIME JUICE	SODA WATER, TO TOP
1 OUNCE DRY VERMOUTH	¾ OUNCE SIMPLE SYRUP (PAGE 332)	**GARNISH** ORANGE SLICE

Add Campari, dry vermouth, lime juice, and simple syrup to a cocktail shaker. Add ice and shake until chilled. Strain over ice into a Collins glass. Top with soda water and garnish with an orange slice.

ROYAL PIMM'S CUP

 | **SERVES 1** |

ERIK ADKINS, SLANTED DOOR, SAN FRANCISCO, CA

Erik Adkins wantonly tosses tradition to the wind in his Royal Pimm's Cup, which is built on a boozy Pimm's mix of his own making. "The idea of blending different vermouths and Amari shows up in Colin Peter Field's book *The Cocktails of the Ritz Paris*," says Adkins. "Summer Cups are blended to order, and then topped lavishly with sparkling wine." Because, as Adkins says, "you can add Champagne to anything and call it 'royal.'"

2½ OUNCES PIMM'S MIX (SEE NOTE) 3 OUNCES SPARKLING WINE	1½ OUNCES GINGER ALE, PREFERABLY FEVER TREE ¼ OUNCE LEMON JUICE	**GARNISH** CUCUMBER, LEMON PEEL, MINT SPRIG, SEASONAL BERRIES

In a 14-ounce Collins glass, combine all ingredients. Add ice and gently stir. Decorate lavishly with cucumber, lemon peel, mint, and berries.

NOTE To make Adkins's Pimm's Mix, combine 6 ounces gin, 6 ounces Campari, 6 ounces sweet vermouth, 6 ounces dry vermouth, 6 ounces Dubonnet, and 3 ounces Punt e Mes in a pitcher and stir well. Makes 1 quart; store in an airtight container in the refrigerator for up to 1 month.

SAKURA MARTINI

 | **SERVES 1** |

KENTA GOTO, BAR GOTO, NEW YORK, NY

In Bar Goto's house martini, a salted cherry blossom is a brilliant and astoundingly beautiful replacement for the hint of saltiness that an olive typically brings. Here, the Martini formula is inverted, with gin acting as an accent to a dry, vinous sake base, combined with maraschino's subtle floral notes and sweetness. Owner Kenta Goto sources the cherry blossoms through a Japanese importer, but you can buy them on Amazon, too.

2½ OUNCES SAKE, PREFERABLY DRY TO MEDIUM BODY	¼ TEASPOON MARASCHINO LIQUEUR, PREFERABLY LUXARDO	**GARNISH** SALTED CHERRY BLOSSOM
1 OUNCE GIN		

Combine all ingredients in a mixing glass. Add ice and stir until chilled. Strain into a coupe and garnish with a salted cherry blossom.

SECOND SERVE

SERVES 1

DAN GREENBAUM, ATTABOY, NEW YORK, NY

As a lower-alcohol, softer-hitting drink, Second Serve, Dan Greenbaum's combination of floral Amaro Montenegro (one of the lighter amari) and salty fino sherry, is a friendly Spain vs. Italy matchup in the form of a savory Collins. "The idea was to make a drink that you could have a few of and not get too drunk," says Greenbaum.

---

1 OUNCE AMARO MONTENEGRO

1 OUNCE FINO SHERRY, PREFERABLY VALDESPINO INOCENTE

1 OUNCE LIME JUICE

¾ OUNCE SIMPLE SYRUP (PAGE 332)

SODA WATER, TO TOP

GARNISH
ORANGE SLICE

Add all ingredients, except soda water, to a cocktail shaker. Shake and strain into an ice-filled Collins glass. Top with soda and garnish with an orange slice.

SHOW ME STATE

 | **SERVES 1** |

ROBERT SACHSE, NITECAP, NEW YORK, NY

Robert Sachse's Show Me State is named for his home state of Missouri. "It was my first drink on a menu in New York and there was a bit of home-state pride on achieving something after moving here," says Sachse. What started as a riff on the Jungle Bird (page 108), a tiki classic, transformed almost entirely: orange juice replaced pineapple juice, Campari was exchanged for mezcal, and dry curaçao replaced the blackstrap rum, turning the Show Me State into a citrus-driven, smoky frozen cocktail all its own.

1½ OUNCES DRY ORANGE CURAÇAO	¾ OUNCE MEZCAL	**GARNISH**
1½ OUNCES ORANGE JUICE	½ OUNCE LIME JUICE	LIME WHEEL AND AN AMERICAN FLAG TOOTHPICK
	½ OUNCE SIMPLE SYRUP (PAGE 332)	

Add all ingredients to a blender with 5 or 6 regular-size ice cubes, cracked. Blend until smooth and pour into a Collins glass. Garnish with a floating lime wheel with an American flag standing ceremoniously on top.

SUPPRESSOR #1

 | **SERVES 1** |

GREG BEST, TICONDEROGA CLUB, ATLANTA, GA

As Ticonderoga Club's Paul Calvert says about drinking Suppressors, "You're between two places, and you just want to hold the line. . . . That feeling could last all night." Fatigued by the trend toward high-alcohol drinks, Calvert and his partner, Greg Best, Atlanta bar legends, went after an entirely different genre of cocktail, setting guidelines for themselves to make drinks "that have delicacy and nuance—the higher-proof shit can't be in there," says Calvert. The perfect version of this is Best's O.G. Suppressor #1, which draws on the most basic building block of low-proof cocktails: fortified wines. Vermouth mixes with the savoriness of sherry and citrus notes to create compelling layers of flavor sans the hard stuff.

---

1 OUNCE DRY VERMOUTH, PREFERABLY DOLIN	1 OUNCE PX SHERRY, PREFERABLY ALVEAR PX 2008	2 BARSPOONS LEMON JUICE
1 OUNCE COCCHI AMERICANO	8 DROPS GRAPEFRUIT BITTERS, PREFERABLY BITTERMENS	**GARNISH** ORANGE PEEL AND MINT SPRIG

Build ingredients over crushed ice in a julep cup. Garnish with an orange peel and a sprig of mint.

TOKYO DRIFT

 | **SERVES 1** |

BRAD FARRAN, BULL DURHAM BEER CO., DURHAM, NC

"There are so many Manhattan variations, but I hadn't seen one done with Japanese whisky yet," says bartender Brad Farran, who devised this drink in 2011 while working at Brooklyn's Clover Club, just as those Japanese imports were beginning to get attention in the States. With this blueprint in mind, Farran substituted the subtly complex Yamazaki for American whiskey, and added spicy Cardamaro to layer a sherry-like note over the vermouth and saffron-infused Strega for a pop of flavor. "I have always loved the challenge of reinventing, updating, or attempting to improve upon a classic," says Farran. "However, I also try whenever doing so not to simply swap out one ingredient for another, dust off my hands, and pat myself on the back, having 'invented' a new drink."

---

2 OUNCES JAPANESE WHISKY, PREFERABLY YAMAZAKI 12-YEAR WHISKY	¾ OUNCE SWEET VERMOUNTH	1 TEASPOON LIQUORE STREGA
	½ OUNCE CARDAMARO	**GARNISH** LEMON PEEL

Add all ingredients to a mixing glass. Add ice and stir until chilled. Strain into a chilled coupe or cocktail glass. Garnish with a lemon peel.

TRIDENT

 | **SERVES 1** |

ROBERT HESS, SEATTLE, WA

The Trident is a nautically inspired interpretation of the Negroni (page 135), created in 2000 by Robert Hess, a cocktail enthusiast from Seattle. In his endeavor to reinterpret the classic, Hess reappointed the Negroni's trifecta of ingredients—strong, bitter, sweet—with distant cousins of the same flavor profiles, each hailing from a seafaring country. Aquavit is swapped in for gin, Cynar for Campari, and sherry for sweet vermouth, with a dash of peach bitters on top. The Trident has become a Seattle staple, enjoying an extended reign at the Zig Zag Café, one of the city's best-known cocktail joints.

---

1 OUNCE AQUAVIT, PREFERABLY LINIE	1 OUNCE FINO SHERRY, PREFERABLY LA INA	**GARNISH** LEMON PEEL
1 OUNCE CYNAR	2 DASHES PEACH BITTERS	

Add all ingredients to a mixing glass. Add ice and stir well. Strain into a chilled coupe or cocktail glass. Garnish with a lemon peel.

WEATHERED AXE

SERVES 1

DANNY SHAPIRO, SCOFFLAW, CHICAGO, IL

Though it may seem like a breezy summer cocktail, with the inclusion of citrusy Combier and herbal-sweet Cocchi Americano, the Weathered Axe easily transitions into a cold-weather drink with the swap of a garnish. This staple at Chicago's Scofflaw is traditionally served with a bouquet of fresh, cooling mint that's hit with a spritz of absinthe, but come January, the evergreen aromatics of rosemary transform the Axe into a savory winter drink.

1½ OUNCES BOURBON, 100 PROOF	½ OUNCE COCCHI AMERICANO	**GARNISH** MINT SPRIG (OR SUBSTITUTE ROSEMARY FOR A SEASONAL WINTERY TOUCH) AND A SPRITZ OF ABSINTHE
¾ OUNCE LEMON JUICE	½ OUNCE GINGER SYRUP (PAGE 333)	
½ OUNCE COMBIER		

Add all ingredients to a cocktail shaker. Add ice and shake until chilled. Strain into a rocks glass over ice. Garnish with a bouquet of mint or a sprig of rosemary and a spritz of absinthe.

WHITE NEGRONI

 | **SERVES 1** |

WAYNE COLLINS, LONDON

It took more than a hundred years for Suze, a fragrant gentian-based French aperitif, to finally make its way to the United States. For years, bartenders were forced to covertly bring it back from trips to Paris in their suitcases. But now that it's been here for a few years, it's become a bit of a bartenders' darling for its light but bitter edge. Suze is often used as a substitute for potent bitters, such as Campari or amaro, to create less assertive, more aromatic drinks. This version of a Negroni (page 135), adapted from London bartender Wayne Collins's riff, turns the original on its head by substituting floral Lillet for sweet vermouth and Suze for the bitter twinge of Campari.

| 1½ OUNCES GIN | ¾ OUNCE SUZE | **GARNISH** |
| | 1 OUNCE LILLET BLANC | LEMON PEEL |

Add all ingredients to a mixing glass. Add ice and stir until chilled. Strain over ice into a rocks glass, or into a chilled coupe or cocktail glass if serving up, if preferred. Garnish with a lemon peel.

WHITE NEGRONI SBAGLIATO

 | **SERVES 1** |

TOBY CECCHINI, LONG ISLAND BAR, BROOKLYN, NY

Legend has it that the Negroni Sbagliato (page 136), a Negroni that subs sparkling wine for gin, was the happy mistake of a Milanese bartender. But as everyone now knows, a great way to improve on any great drink is to spritz it. There's no mistake here, as herbal Suze meets bianco vermouth in Toby Cecchini's sbagliato version of the modern classic White Negroni (page 327).

1 OUNCE SUZE	4 OUNCES SPARKLING WINE, PREFERABLY PROSECCO	**GARNISH** LONG SLICE OF CUCUMBER AND ORANGE PEEL
1 OUNCE BIANCO VERMOUTH, PREFERABLY CARPANO		

Build ingredients over a large cube in a double old-fashioned or Collins glass. Garnish with a long slice of cucumber and an orange peel.

WHITE RUSSIAN

 | **SERVES 1**

TOBY CECCHINI, LONG ISLAND BAR, BROOKLYN, NY

Called simply "the Russian," the earliest incarnation of this drink (c. 1930) lacked its now-signature coffee liqueur; not until its heyday in the 1960s did a version with Kahlua rise to prominence. For more recent generations, the drink achieved cult status not for its flavor, but due to its supporting role in *The Big Lebowski*, as the signature of Jeff Bridges' character the Dude. This recipe, from famed New York bartender Toby Cecchini, calls for not one but two coffee liqueurs, and kicks it up even further by whipping the cream that is typically stirred in, and floating it atop the drink.

4 OUNCES HEAVY CREAM	2 OUNCES VODKA OR RUM, PREFERABLY ABSOLUT ELYX VODKA OR PLANTATION 5-YEAR BARBADOS GRANDE RÉSERVE RUM	½ OUNCE KAHLÚA
¼ OUNCE AMARETTO, PREFERABLY LUXARDO AMARETTO DI SASCHIRA		½ OUNCE TOSCHI NOCELLO
		1 OUNCE COFFEE LIQUEUR, PREFERABLY HOUSE SPIRITS

Add heavy cream and amaretto to a shaker. Add the coil of a Hawthorne strainer and dry shake for 10 seconds or so, to aerate but not whip into stiffness. Add remaining ingredients to another cocktail shaker with ice and shake until chilled. Strain into a coupe or rocks glass. Holding a slotted spoon closely over the surface of the drink, pour a finger's worth of cream through it to float atop the drink.

syrups

SIMPLE SYRUP

MAKES ABOUT
1¼ CUPS

1 CUP WHITE,
CANE OR
DEMERARA
SUGAR

1 CUP WATER

Combine sugar and water in a small saucepan over low heat. Stir until the sugar is completely dissolved and remove from the heat. Allow to cool to room temperature before transferring to a jar. Syrup will keep in the refrigerator for 1 month.

RICH SIMPLE SYRUP

MAKES ABOUT
2 CUPS

2 CUPS CANE
OR DEMERARA
SUGAR

1 CUP WATER

Combine sugar and water in a small saucepan over low heat. Stir until sugar is completely dissolved and remove from the heat. Allow to cool to room temperature before transferring to a jar. Syrup will keep in the refrigerator for 1 month.

HONEY SYRUP

MAKES ABOUT
1½ CUPS

1 CUP HONEY

½ CUP WATER

Combine honey and water in a small saucepan over low heat. Stir until honey is completely dissolved and remove from the heat. Allow to cool to room temperature before transferring to a jar. Syrup will keep in the refrigerator for 1 month.

GINGER SYRUP

MAKES ABOUT
2⅓ CUPS

1 RECIPE RICH
SIMPLE SYRUP,
WARM

⅓ CUP PURE
GINGER JUICE

Combine simple syrup and ginger juice in an airtight container and stir. Chill before using. Syrup will keep in the refrigerator for 2 weeks.

CINNAMON SYRUP

MAKES ABOUT
1¼ CUPS

1 CUP SUGAR

1 CUP WATER

2-INCH-LONG
CINNAMON
STICK

Combine sugar, water, and cinnamon stick in a small saucepan over low heat. Stir until sugar is completely dissolved and remove from the heat. Let stand overnight, then strain and discard cinnamon stick and transfer to a jar. Syrup will keep in the refrigerator for 1 month.

GRENADINE

MAKES 1 QUART

3 CUPS
POMEGRANATE
JUICE

2 CUPS SUGAR

PINCH OF SALT

PEEL OF
1 ORANGE

Heat 2 cups of the pomegranate juice in a saucepan over medium heat. Bring to a boil, then lower the heat and simmer until the volume is reduced by half. Add remaining 1 cup pomegranate juice and sugar and continue to simmer, stirring, until sugar has dissolved. Remove from the heat and add salt and orange peel, expressing the peel (twisting to release oils) into the liquid before adding the whole pieces. Cool completely and remove peels before using. Grenadine will keep in the refrigerator for 2 weeks.

index

Published in the United States by Ten Speed Press, an
imprint of the Crown Publishing Group, a division of
Penguin Random House LLC, New York.

www.crownpublishing.com
www.tenspeed.com

Ten Speed Press and the Ten Speed Press colophon are
registered trademarks of Penguin Random House LLC.

Library of Congress Cataloging-in-Publication Data
is on file with the publisher.

Hardcover ISBN: 978-0-39957-931-8
eBook ISBN: 978-0-39957-932-5

Printed in China

Design by Margaux Keres

14